The Journey of Life

The Journey of Life

Dr. Glen Martin
and the
Journey of Faith Pastoral Staff

CROSSBOOKS
PUBLISHING

CrossBooks™
A Division of LifeWay
1663 Liberty Drive
Bloomington, IN 47403
www.crossbooks.com
Phone: 1-866-879-0502

First published by CrossBooks 8/25/2011

ISBN: 978-1-4627-0520-7 (sc)
ISBN: 978-1-4627-0521-4 (hc)

Printed in the United States of America

This book is printed on acid-free paper.

To our visionary and sacrificial brothers and sisters
who accepted God's call one hundred years ago
to start Community Baptist Church.
Well done, good and faithful servants;
we thank you.

Contents

About the Authors

Dr. Glen Martin: Since 1991, Glen has been the senior pastor of Journey of Faith in Manhattan Beach, California. He has written twelve books for pastors and leaders, several of which have been translated into Indonesian, Chinese, and Korean. Besides serving as a speaker and seminar leader for Promise Keepers, INJOY, and Man in the Mirror, Glen has taught at numerous seminaries across the United States and around the world. Glen's postgraduate education includes a master's degree in Christian education and a doctor of ministry, both from Talbot School of Theology, as well as a master of theology degree from Western Seminary. His passion is to teach the Scriptures, to equip the church to reach the lost, and to mobilize the body of believers to achieve its full potential. Glen stays energized with reading, visiting historical sites, and taking long walks with his wife, Nancy. They are blessed with three grown children and four grandchildren.

Pastor Bill Ingram: Joining the staff of Journey of Faith in 2007, Bill serves as chief of staff and pastor of outreach ministries, which includes long- and short-term mission trips as well as local outreach. He has degrees from Southern California College (Vanguard University) and Hope International University, where he earned his master's in 2009. In addition to Bill's drive to see people become "missional" with their lives, he is motivated to help singles connect to God and develop healthy relationships with one another. He is married to Denise and has four children—Amber, Tyler, Drew, and Isaac. Besides reading and playing with their children, Bill and his wife love to golf; one item on his "bucket list" is to golf in all fifty states and on every continent.

Pastor Harry McFarlin: After being the pastor to older adults at Journey for eight years and assistant pastor part time for seven years, Harry continues to minister to older adults through teaching, traveling, and advising. After his graduation from Western Conservative Baptist Seminary in Portland, Oregon, Harry pastored two churches for a total of eighteen years before coming to Journey in 1996. A critical area of his ministry is assisting people who struggle with generational changes. Harry's own life transitions and those of his wife, Donna, continue to inspire him to seek God's message for older adults as they adapt to an ever-changing walk with their Creator. Harry's hope is that this book will challenge us to experience the transitions of life in a new and exciting way. He and Donna have four children and eight grandchildren.

Dr. Jason Cusick: Jason joined the Journey of Faith staff in 2004. He has a master's degree in Christian ministry and leadership and a doctor of ministry from Talbot School of Theology. Coming from a ministry in hospital chaplaincy, Jason has served Journey as pastor of care ministries and pastor of adult discipleship. He has also overseen Journey's Premarital Mentoring Program and the Journey Leadership Institute. In addition, he has brought Griefshare, Care Groups, and Stephen Ministry to Journey of Faith. He has a passion for helping individuals and couples work through their challenges to find God's best for their lives. Jason has been married to his college sweetheart, Marie, for more than fifteen years, and they have three children. He is a published author, and when he is not teaching, writing, and caring for others, he loves sharing his opinions about the latest movies and pop culture news.

Pastor Greg Piken: Greg is passionate about helping others discover who they are in Christ. He prays to see church members step out in faith to lead revolutionary lives for God in their careers and schools, among the poor, and around the world. After recording and releasing three independent albums as a singer and songwriter, Greg joined the Journey of Faith staff in December 2004. He earned his M.A. in biblical and theological studies from Talbot School of Theology at Biola University, and his B.A. in English and comparative literature from University of California at Irvine. Currently, he oversees the ever-growing ministries of college students, young adults, and singles as he fulfills the call of God upon his life.

Pastor Mark Portis: Mark is the pastor of worship arts at Journey of Faith. His calling and desire is to help God's people passionately and authentically offer their worship to God both corporately and personally. Mark graduated from Cal State Fullerton in 1989 with a bachelor's degree in music. After his position as a worship leader at Rolling Hills Covenant Church from 1990 to 1993, he served eleven years at Lake Avenue Church in Pasadena as a pastor of worship before coming to Journey of Faith in 2005. He and his wife, Linda, have been married twenty years and have three sons—Kevin, John, and Michael. Mark has been on the adjunct faculty at Azusa Pacific University and is a sought-after worship leader for conference centers such as Mount Hermon and Forest Home. In his spare time, Mark enjoys bike riding, tennis, watching good movies, writing and arranging music, and spending time with his family.

Pastor Claire Abernathy: Claire has been on staff at Journey of Faith since 1998. As the children's pastor, she longs to see kids not only discover God's amazing love for them, but also develop a thriving relationship with their Savior. Raised in a secular home, Claire understands that regardless of what family you come from, God has great plans for you if you will seek Him with all your heart. When a high school friend invited her to youth group, it changed her life; she discovered what it meant to belong to a church family. Claire earned her undergraduate degree from Cal State University at Long Beach and is pursuing a degree in Christian education from Talbot School of Theology. Claire and her husband, Jim, have three children and live in Torrance, California.

Pastor Michelle Browne: When Michelle was attending Slippery Rock Baptist Camp in Pennsylvania at age eleven, God called her to work with teenagers. Michelle pursued that dream, serving as a youth ministries volunteer and working with teenagers for the past eighteen years. She graduated with a bachelor's degree in religious education from Davis College in Johnson City, New York, and taught school with her husband, Jerry, in Medina, Ohio. In 2011, they will celebrate their fifteenth anniversary. Michelle considers herself honored to have served the amazing students and families at Journey of Faith since joining the staff in 2005. She plans to pursue a master's degree in the near future.

Pastor Matt Johnston: Matt has been on staff as high school pastor at Journey of Faith since 2010. Born and raised in Southern California, Matt earned a degree in Christian education from Biola University and has served in youth ministry since 2003. His experience has provided him with a unique perspective on both shepherding and parenting teens. Seeing so many different types of families and parenting styles in action, Matt shares his objective insight on raising teenagers through a turbulent yet pivotal time of life. In their spare time, he and his wife, Caroline, enjoy reading, traveling, exploring the South Bay, and being devoted Dodgers fans.

Dr. Don Willett: Don came to Journey in 2003 with a ministry that focuses on discipling adults toward ongoing spiritual growth. Don's enthusiasm for ministry to men and the development of small groups gave rise to Men Made New, an avenue for transformation and growth for men and their families on their journey of faith. In 2008, Pastor Don became the campus pastor of Journey of Faith, Bellflower, a satellite and partner of Journey of Faith, Manhattan Beach. Don completed his Ph.D. in educational studies at Talbot School of Theology in 1997 after receiving a master's degree in divinity and one in Christian education. Together, Don and his wife, Barbara, have three grown children and three grandchildren. Don's spare time is spent visiting family, enjoying sports, reading, and developing friendships.

Acknowledgments

The mission statement of Journey of Faith Church is clear and vibrant and has motivated the direction and impact of this Body of Believers for 100 years:

> As a community of worshipers
> We have been sent into the world
> To MAKE, MATURE and MOBILIZE disciples
> Who love the Lord God above all else,
> And who touch others with the reality of Jesus Christ.

To accomplish this mission, the staff has worked synergistically to create both continuity and unity in the church. God also raised up a team of people to assist the staff in many of Journey's major projects. This book represents one of these significant projects. So …

1. Special thanks to all Journey staff for their diligence and expertise in the writing of their chapters.
2. Special thanks to Nancy Martin for compiling the different texts and skillfully formatting each chapter to fit within the general guidelines for submission.
3. Special thanks to Laura Mecoy and Cary Walker, whose editing skills and keen eye shaped the book into something greater than the sum of its parts or chapters.
4. Special thanks to Jon Crowe for designing the cover. His creative expression is a joy to work with and a great gift to the kingdom.

5. Special thanks to Emily Brantley for your drawings, which became part of the very fabric of the message of the book.
6. Special thanks to Vicky Gallion for adding some strategic graphics and internally taking the text to a new level of presentation and desirability.

Journey of Faith Church ... we love you. We are honored to serve you ... and we are blessed to have you call us your pastors.

The Journey Staff

1

The Journey Begins

Glen Martin

God is there through all the seasons of life
we encounter. Not only does God determine
whether or not there is life, but He also
determines what that life will become.

None of us likes to be confronted with the arithmetic of life. Mortality is a very private matter, and how dare anyone intrude into an area so sacred and scary. But the Bible does just that. Psalm 90:12 finds God saying, "Teach us to number our days aright, that we may gain a heart of wisdom." When you're young and read this passage, you tend to fly right past it, missing out on the significance and relevancy. But at middle age, the threats increase, and we begin to focus on the task. "Nope; I don't want to take a hard look at life's time line; it's a waste of my time and my emotions. Besides, whatever happened to those feelings of invincibility I used to have?"

The Bible says that I have seventy to eighty years of life to live (Psalm 90:10ab). Some are blessed with more; some less. As I sit down to write this chapter, I have just turned fifty-seven. Let's see—eighty minus fifty-seven, times 365 days; that leaves me with about 8,395 days, plus or minus, left. Ah, I feel better. That is a long time, even in dog years. I have plenty of time left to accomplish all I want with the last quarter of my life. Maybe this arithmetic of life is not all that daunting after all. Unfortunately, from everything I read and hear, time seems to speed up with age. No, the cosmic order of the time-space continuum is not transformed. But the "other side of the hill" appears a bit more slippery than the climb, and we begin to notice the rate increase emotionally and psychologically.

I was born September 3, 1953, in a small town outside of London. And one day, my numbering of days will reach a conclusion; let's say in 2033 after an eighty-year run. My three wonderful kids and multiple grandchildren will choose a coffin and a suitable plaque to mark the place where my ashes await a reunion with my new body to live eternally in heaven. Somewhere on the plaque will be the date I was born and the date I breathed my last breath, with a "dash" separating the two. In eternity, what will matter most is not the date my life started or the date my life ended. What will matter most is what I did with my "dash." And in the time we have with breath—whether that be twenty-three years, sixty-three years, or three weeks—we are going to be given the chance to really live life the way God intended us to enjoy the seasons of life, as some of the ancients wrote, or the "Passages" described by noted author Gail Sheehy. That's what you are going to learn in this book.

Life is a series of seasons and transitions, and these different periods of life are not always linear. Please realize that as we think about the journey of life, we're not necessarily talking about a chronological matrix when family leads to salvation and on to marriage, kids, a job, a trial or two, retirement and a gold watch, and, alas, heaven. What we share in this book is not necessarily chronological. As a matter of fact, these seasons are normally *not* chronological. Sometimes, we can be in one or more of these seasons at a time. This book is a discussion of some of the general characteristics we find ourselves enjoying or enduring, and the lessons God wants us to learn along the way. This book also offers guidance on two imperatives for all the seasons of the Christian life—prayer and worship. Our goal is to help equip you for the journey of life and ensure that you find the spiritual healing that is available in every season. That is what I hope we can accomplish together in this book as the staff of Journey of Faith walks with you through this study completed in 2011.

The Uniqueness of Human Life

As we begin our study of the journey of life, I will start at the very beginning, realizing that it can no longer be taken for granted that everybody accepts the "uniqueness" or "value" of human life. We have become a throwaway culture that diminishes human life by means of a convenient procedure with the inherent value of a problem easily solved. But ideas have consequences, and the idea that human beings are nothing more than another form of biological life has consequences.

Many of the more troubling aspects of modern life ultimately stem from a lessening of the priority of human life. On the other hand, a proper view of ourselves as unique creatures of God ought to have a very positive effect on our conduct and, especially, on our treatment of others. So a bigger question must be answered as we begin our journey of life: "What is God's view of life?" or "How will God's view of life change the way we live our journey of life?" Several biblical principles become paramount in our understanding.

First, from the very beginning, the story of creation demonstrates the high value God places on human life. Early in the Scriptures, we are told the following:

Then God said, "Let us make man in our image, in our likeness, and let them rule over the fish of the sea and the birds of the air, over the livestock, over all the earth, and over all the creatures that move along the ground." So God created man in his own image, in the image of God he created him; male and female he created them. God blessed them and said to them, "Be fruitful and increase in number; fill the earth and subdue it. Rule over the fish of the sea and the birds of the air and over every living creature that moves on the ground" (Genesis 1:26–28).

God created man—not random mutations or evolutionary processes. Genesis 2:7 goes on to say, "The LORD God formed the man from the dust of the ground and breathed into his nostrils the breath of life, and the man became a living being." Man did not evolve from a single-celled organism over the span of millions of years; he is the special creation of God. The fact that God singled out man for special care in creation lets us know that there is a vast difference between humans and the rest of the animal kingdom.

God Created Us to Be Spiritual Beings

Here is one of the greatest dangers in the teaching of evolution as it is taught to our children in public schools. If people can be convinced that they are nothing more than the product of random selection, human life loses all value. We need to remember that every human is a special creation of God Himself! And why? Because God created us to be spiritual beings. We are told man was made *in the image* of God. This does not mean we look like God, or that God has a body like we do. It does mean we were created like God in that we are tripartite beings. In the Godhead, there is the Father, the Son, and the Spirit. In us, there is the body, the soul, and the spirit. This is the primary way in which humankind can be distinguished from the other members of the animal kingdom.

Let's take just a moment to examine each of these parts. The body is the vehicle with which we move through and interact with our world. It is the body that provides a home for the soul and the spirit while we are in this world. Both humans and animals have bodies. When we die, our bodies return to the earth. Genesis 3:19 makes this clear in saying, " 'By the sweat of your brow you will eat your food until you return to the ground, since from it you were taken; for dust you are and to dust you will return.' "

But God does make a distinction between body, soul, and spirit for good reason. The soul is the seat of the will, the character, the intellect, the thoughts, and the emotions. The soul is where we reason, love, hate, want, and so on. The soul is what we refer to when we speak of the mind. Your soul animates your body and allows your body to interact with your world and with other people. In short, your soul is that part of you that makes you who you are. Your soul makes you self-conscious.

As we turn our attention to the spirit, this is where the similarities between man and animals end forever. Whereas the soul makes us self-conscious, the spirit allows us to be God-conscious. Every person born into this world is born spiritually dead. The apostle Paul, in writing to the small band of believers in ancient Ephesus, wanted them to grasp the implications of living their lives "in Christ." In speaking about the initial transformation that takes place in everyone who surrenders their life to Christ, Paul shares, "As for you, you were dead in your transgressions and sins, in which

The fact that God singled out man for special care in creation lets us know that there is a vast difference between humans and the rest of the animal kingdom.

you used to live when you followed the ways of this world and of the ruler of the kingdom of the air, the spirit who is now at work in those who are disobedient" (Ephesians 2:1–2). But, when the spirit of God begins to draw a person toward salvation, He brings to life the spirit that is within a man, and this person finds his spirit reaching out in faith toward God. After salvation, the new spirit of life within a person begins to transform the soul part of man. And these changes within the spirit and the soul demonstrate themselves in the action of the body, the physical dwelling God provided for our brief tenure on earth.

This can be a bit complicated, but think of it like this: the "soul" and the "spirit" are similar in the manner in which they are used in the spiritual life of the believer. They are different in their reference. The "soul" is our horizontal view with the world. The "spirit" is our vertical view with God. It is important to understand that both refer to the immaterial part of us, but only the "spirit" refers to our walk with God. The "soul" refers to our walk in the world. When we leave this world, the soul and spirit return to God to be dealt with accordingly. Ecclesiastes 12:7 says, "And the dust returns to the ground it came from, and the spirit returns to God who gave it." The redeemed go to glory (John 14:1–3); the lost to hell (Psalm 9:17; 2 Thessalonians 1:8–9).

God Is in Control of Our Journey

We are the special creation of God. We were made in the image of God, and we have the capacity to know God. All prove we are special creatures in the eyes of the Lord. They also establish the fact that God is sovereign over the creation of human life and is in control of our journey of life—not us. It is God's sovereignty and power that ultimately determines life from birth to death.

The creation of life is far more than the physical union between a man and a woman. Ask Leah and Rachel, whose stories are told in the book of Genesis, as Moses writes, "When the LORD saw that Leah was not loved, he opened her womb, but Rachel was barren" (Genesis 29:31). Ask Rachel, who cried out for God's intervention and "… God remembered Rachel; he listened to her and opened her womb" (Genesis 30:22). In every situation, the sovereign God was working behind the scenes to determine whether or not an egg was fertilized. He determines whether or not life begins. Now, I realize there are often physical issues involved in conception as well. Still, behind it all is the sovereign will of God. He opens the womb, and He closes the womb according to His will.

God is there through all the seasons of life we encounter. Not only does God determine whether or not there is life, but He also determines what that life will become. He has a plan for every human. The Bible tells us God had His hand on Jeremiah and even had a plan for the prophet's life before he was born. Jeremiah 1:5 says, " 'Before I formed you in the womb I knew you, before you were born I set you apart; I appointed you as a prophet to the nations.' " What you and I are in this life is not the product of random chance and hapless genetics. What we are in this life is a product of divine sovereignty.

This was the conviction of David, which is recorded in Psalm 139:13–16:

> For you created my inmost being; you knit me together in my mother's womb. I praise you because I am fearfully and wonderfully made; your works are wonderful, I know that full well. My frame was not hidden from you when I was made in the secret place. When I was woven together in the depths of the earth, your eyes saw my unformed body. All the days ordained for me were written in your book before one of them came to be.

David recognized God's power and involvement in his life from the very beginning. Steven Lawson, well-known pastor and author, shares, "This is proven in that the Lord has made him skillfully in his mother's womb. God created his inmost being (i.e., his kidneys, symbolic of his vital organs, his heart, liver, lungs, even his innermost emotions and moral sensitivities). God knit him like a skilled artisan would weave a beautiful tapestry."[1]

Trust God Through Life's Trials

Among the goals for this book is awakening sensitivity within you to God's leading in each of the seasons of life. Watch for and submit to God's hand in your family as you seek to become better stewards of your children who have been entrusted to you. Remember your commitments to God when you become disillusioned with dating and purity or your marriage. It is God who guides. If you have made a vow to Him, He expects you to keep it. Trust God through the trials of life, the growing pains of life, and the ebb and flow of your career. Your personal journey will include significant seasons where God is molding you into the man or woman He wants you to become. And remember, just as surely as the Lord God Almighty is sovereign in the creation of life and the journey of life, two issues become very clear from the Bible.

First, God determines the arithmetic of life. This is the clear teaching of Job, where we learn in Job 14:5, " 'Man's days are determined; you have decreed the number of his months and have set limits he cannot exceed.' "

Just as surely as the Lord has a plan regarding the beginning and the middle of your life, He has a plan for the end of your life as well. Hebrews 9:27 is not subtle in proclaiming, "Just as man is destined to die once, and after that to face judgment." God knows the day, the hour, the minute, even the very second when you will breathe your last and you will enter the eternity you have chosen.

God Should Determine the Journey's End

Second, it is God who should determine when the journey is over. Man is assuming the place of God when he reaches out to take another human being's life, whether we are talking about murder, suicide, euthanasia, or abortion. As God has planned it, you will leave this world exactly when, where, and how the Lord has predetermined it. It was the Lord's will that Moses die alone with God on a mountain according to Deuteronomy 34:5–8. It was God's will that Jacob die surrounded by his children, according to Genesis 49:33. It was God's will that Paul die at the hands of Roman executioners. Sometimes people leave through tragedies. Sometimes people die because of disease. Sometimes they pass away from old age. Sometimes they go suddenly with the bloom of youth still on their cheeks. However they leave this world, it is God's will that must determine the *when,* the *where,* and the *how*—not the will of men. Now, please don't misunderstand me. There are times when it becomes necessary to withhold further medical treatment and just allow nature to take its course. I have had to make these types of decisions and help families do the same. You have not committed murder; you have simply placed the matter into God's hands. However, to put a helpless, voiceless baby to death because he or she is an inconvenience is biblically unacceptable!

A Brief Word About Evolution

An overview book such as this one does not permit me space or time for a defense of creationism over evolution. But anyone reading this book must at least wrestle with the question "How did life first appear?" And here is where the armies of the evolutionists and creationists have blasted away with considerably more noise than skill, producing more heat than light.

In reality, you have two presuppositions to choose from. Life is either (1) a cosmic accident with no rhyme or reason to what happens, other than survival of the fittest and evolutionary progress, or (2) life is the result of intelligent design where a person can detect a designer simply by examining the evidence of the design. Those are your two choices!

With respect to the origin of life, Charles Darwin claimed he knew the answer. He said it was all by evolution from a single cell existing in the primordial ooze, which, by a process of division and mutation, ultimately resulted in the many groups and forms of life we find today. But many scientists now confess great uneasiness with this theory. Some flatly admit that it is no longer believable as Darwin envisioned it. Why? Because Darwin's Law of Natural Selection has much to say about how different species evolved. But his law has nothing to say about the root of life or the DNA of life. How did it all begin? A. S. Romer, writing in the book *Man and the Vertebrates,* says, "We have no certain fossil record of lower chordates [animals with backbones] or chordate ancestors, and very possibly never shall have. The oldest ancestors of the vertebrates are unknown and they may always remain unknown."[2] These words are rather startling when we face the widespread allegiance to Darwinian evolution that exists in the popular mind today. But the Bible, even at the beginning, addresses this great question of the mystery of origin and proposes a solution science cannot discount: God created the heavens and the earth.

Intelligent Design at Work

Years ago, we took a family vacation to the Black Hills of South Dakota. Driving through the expanse of this pristine landscape is breathtaking. Our final destination on this scenic drive, however, was Mount Rushmore. Same landscape. Same geology. One significant difference: intelligent design. Someone—specifically Gutzon Borglum and, later, his son, Lincoln Borglum, changed the landscape and altered this mountain. When you make your way from the parking lot to the entrance and gaze upon the four giant presidents carved into the side of this mountain, you immediately know: Someone knew what they were doing. Someone designed this!

The same is true in the design of life. I believe William Dembski, world-renowned mathematician, philosopher, and author, got it right in his excellent work, *Intelligent Design:*

> Creation is a gift. What's more, it is a gift of the most important thing we possess—ourselves. Indeed creation is the means by which a creator—divine, human or otherwise—gives oneself in self-revelation. Creation is not the neurotic, forced self-revelation offered on the psychoanalyst's couch. Nor is it the facile self-revelation of idle chatter. It is the self-revelation of labor and sacrifice. Creation always incurs a cost. Creation invests the creator's life in the thing created. When God creates humans, he breathes into them the breath of life—God's own life. At the end of the six days of creation God is tired—He has to rest. Creation is exhausting work. It is drawing oneself out of oneself and then imprinting oneself on the other.[3]

God Is the Inescapable One

We can never escape the thought of God. There has never been a society or civilization discovered on the face of the earth that does not have a concept of God and worship. We are irrepressibly worshipful beings. We must worship something, and the reason for this is very simple. It is because everything around us and within us speaks of the existence of another personality, a being of great intelligence, power, and wisdom, who must exist somewhere. We can never escape that thought. It is only the power of rationalization that allows us to rid ourselves of the idea of God. We live out our days, the Bible says, within the boundaries of God. God stands at the end of every path we travel and also at the beginning. As Paul said to the intellectuals on Mars Hill in Athens, Acts 17:28a, " 'For in him we live and move and have our being.' "

Ultimately, God is the Inescapable One. Men and women of science explore the atom and come at last to a realm of mystery, where everything is reduced to pure energy, and they do not know what to do with it or what to call it. The astronomers probe into space. They discover the great galaxies whirling in their courses. They see no observable limit to it, but find it all is permeated with tremendous power and energy. They do not know what to label it. The doctor holds a newborn baby in his arms. He cannot explain where life came from, what made it develop in the way it did to produce this little creature. It is all a mystery. We are surrounded by mystery! Such is the journey of life.

Lift Our Voices for God's View of Life

Human life is precious! Human life has value! It is so precious that God sent His Son, Jesus, into this world to save life through His death on the cross. John 3:16–17 says, " 'For God so loved the world that he gave his one and only Son, that whoever believes in him shall not perish but have eternal life. For God did not send his Son into the world to condemn the world, but to save the world through him.' " God values each and every person, but our society does not.

We need to pray for our nation and for our world. America has taken the first steps down a slippery slope that will lead us farther and farther away from God. We have witnessed the dawn of a new day in our country where, in the long run, no one may be safe without a change in the philosophy and definition of life. We need to take our stand, cast our votes, and lift our voices in favor of God's view of life.

Questions to Ponder and Discuss

1. When the Bible tells us to number our days in Psalm 90:12, what is the wisdom to be gained in thinking about the journey of life? What lessons do you believe God wants us to learn on this journey? In your current season of life, what is God teaching you?

2. Considering the times of scientific breakthrough and research, what views of life's origins have you heard being promoted? Why do you think it is so difficult for people to accept the possibility of creationism?

3. An incorrect view of the value of life will affect both ends of the age spectrum. Can you see any signs in today's culture pointing to less care for the elderly and a feeling that the "old" are in the way?

4. Has this chapter changed any of your views on life? What can you do politically, socially, or personally to promote God's view of life?

5. Read Jeremiah 1:5 again. Write a brief description of the implications of this verse for your life.

Recommended Reading

The Case for a Creator by Lee Strobel
For Men: *The Seven Seasons of a Man's Life* by Patrick Morley
New Passages by Gail Sheehy

The Journey Continues ... After starting our journey, we must next understand how God designed us to be relational beings. We are not created to live life in isolation. We are born into a family. Thus, we continue our journey examining the lifelong season of family—beginning with "the ones you got."

2

Family:
Making God the Center of Your Home

Claire Abernathy

If you are a child of God, you should recognize that you also have a responsibility to make sure God is present in your family's home.

You are sitting in your family's festively decorated home early one Christmas morning. There is a familiar holiday song playing softly in the background and the smell of your mom's homemade cinnamon rolls wafting into the living room. Sharing special moments together that are based on your Christian values is not a tradition, but a lifestyle. This is what family has been to you for as long as you can remember. There have been highs and lows, excitement and struggles, baptisms and funerals, milestones and setbacks. But is this homey scene what family is all about? Is this what you will strive for when you have a family of your own, or is this the model you have already chosen for your family?

In this chapter, our goal is to explore the biblical view of family in the context of today's world, to provide spiritual guidance for grappling with the struggles that are inherent in family, and to help you find healing as you cope with the "family you got."

What Is Family?

So what is family? Is it a mom and a dad raising 2.5 children in a two-story house with a picket fence? When does one person become a member of his or her own family, not the one they were born into? Does a family require children? In our own minds, the answer to these questions may well depend on what generation we were born in or lived through.

For baby boomers, family may look like the nuclear families portrayed in the popular television shows of the 1950s and 1960s. They were *The Adventures of Ozzie and Harriet, Father Knows Best,* or *Leave It to Beaver* families in which the father was the sole financial support, working outside the home. The mother stayed at home, baking and cleaning and raising two or three children.

These images of family began to change with *My Three Sons* and the Cartwrights of *Bonanza* fame. Here, we saw men raising their sons alone, their wives having died. *Bonanza* depicted an even greater leap from the nuclear family. Each of the three sons had a different mother, and each mother had died. By the late 1960s and early 1970s, *The Brady Bunch* television show gave us a widower with three boys married to a widow with three girls. We laughed and related to what a big household was like, where not everything went as planned.

In each of these shows, no matter what the obstacles or challenges, all were resolved in less than an hour with love and patience. These are hardly the scenes we see playing out in many American families today. Compare the shows of the fifties and sixties to what is currently viewed by Americans. Some of today's shows, like some of today's families, have strayed far from the traditional model of decades past. Traditional family roles are not dependent on Mom, Dad, and the kids, but have been redefined by the sexuality and gender preferences of the characters. These character portrayals are thought by some to bring depth, complexity, and reality to television, thereby appealing to a more diverse cross section of society. With these new characters comes the acknowledgment of ongoing struggles and issues such as acceptance by their family and their peers. This is a far cry from the scenarios of decades past. In their thirty-minute time slot, the Beaver's parents never had to contend with anything more serious than a neighbor's broken window. The father who knew best never had to grapple with elderly parents who could no longer care for themselves, and Ozzie and Harriet never considered divorce.

These and many other challenges, conflicts, and obstacles are what we often find in the "families we got." When we face these challenges, how can we effectively cope with a family that looks much more like one of today's reality shows than Ozzie and Harriet?

The Blueprint for Family Life

First, as Christians, we need to realize that the entertainment industry does not hold the blueprint for family life. The Bible does. It shows us that our current family and our ancestors of generations past are important as well as diverse. When we read the genealogy of our Lord in Matthew 1, we see that Jesus's earthly ancestors, men and women, were not perfect, yet they were all used by God. Sometimes they were faithful, such as when Abraham prepared to sacrifice his son, Isaac, as a burnt offering or Rahab, as her fear of the Lord and love for her family compelled her to hide Joshua's spies. In cases such as these, it is easy for us to say that our Father in heaven does indeed know best.

Of course that doesn't mean everything will always work out the way we want it to. Look at Joseph and his dysfunctional brothers. I'm sure he enjoyed the love and attention he received from his father, until the jealousy and envy of his brothers changed his life forever. The family he thought loved him unconditionally sold him for twenty pieces of silver. " 'Come, let's sell him to the Ishmaelites and not lay our hands on him; after all, he is our brother, our own flesh and blood' " (Genesis 37:27). What about the role of the father in the Bible? God showed us through Eli that the father is responsible for the actions of his sons. " 'For I told him that I would judge his family forever because of the sin he knew about; his sons made themselves contemptible, and he failed to restrain them' " (1 Samuel 3:13). God's judgment on Eli did not mean he would not be used by God. Eli's mentoring and influence on Samuel, though, would one day lead to the selection of David as king, as a man after God's own heart.

These examples of families in the Bible show us that things don't always work out the way we would hope. There will be many tears—and even more prayers—as we seek God's will in our present circumstances. His Word tells us that no matter how busy we are, and how hectic life is, our Father is there for us. "This is the confidence we have in approaching God: that if we ask anything according to his will, he hears us" (1 John 5:14).

Acknowledging this as individuals, we must admit that some things are out of our control. For this is not the family you chose; it is the family that God chose for you! You did not marry into it or find it on the Internet. You realized one day that you were a son or daughter of God. As you grew physically and mentally, you also grew in your understanding of God and His role in your home. A little later in this book, you will read about the family you choose as it pertains to marriage and parenting. For now, let's look at the family we have, not by our choice but by God's design.

Biblical Descriptions of Family

When we look to the Old Testament for our understanding of family, we come across a couple of terms. The first is *mishpachah*, a Hebrew term referring to a family or clan.[4] This word appears hundreds of times in the Old Testament. It gives us a basis for how we view our extended family more than it does our current nuclear family. In the Old Testament, a clan was a group of people united by a blood lineage. It was used in reference to the extended family. This term was not limited to describing family but was also used to describe a type or kind, as in Genesis 8:19, "All the animals and all the creatures that move along the ground and all the birds—everything that moves on the earth—came out of the ark, one *kind* after another."

The next term referring to family is *patria*.[5] It is a Greek term found in the New Testament. It is broader than the previous reference, as it would include not only a lineage, as in the family of David, but our relation to our heavenly Father when we became part of God's family: "For this reason I kneel before the Father, from whom his whole *family* in heaven and on earth derives its name" (Ephesians 3:14–15). We derive the term *patriarch* from this root, and thus find the link between our earliest views of the family as that which is led by the father.

Family Starts with Our Father in Heaven

Before there was a father on earth, there was and always has been our Father in heaven. We read of God's existence before creation in both the Old and New Testaments.

> In the beginning God created the heavens and the earth. Now the earth was formless and empty, darkness was over the surface of the deep, and the Spirit of God was hovering over the waters (Genesis 1:1–2).

> In the beginning was the Word, and the Word was with God, and the Word was God. He was with God in the beginning. Through him all things were made; without him nothing was made that has been made (John 1:1–3).

God existed in the three persons of the Trinity: Father, Son, and Spirit. Within the Trinity, the Father has the unique role as architect, designer, and creator. It is the Father's position and authority that makes Him supreme among the persons of the Godhead and our role model for the head of the household in the traditional family.

God's creation of man and then woman was the beginning of what would become family here on earth. They were created to be in relationships not only with each other but also with their heavenly Father. They were the first husband and wife, and God gave them specific commands for how they were to live. "God blessed them and said to them, 'Be fruitful and increase in number; fill the earth and subdue it. Rule over the fish of the sea and the birds of the air and over every living creature that moves on the ground' " (Genesis 1:28).

Unfortunately, during the patriarchal period of Abraham, the influences of other cultures led to the practice of polygamy. But this was never intended to be the foundation for the family. The traditional roles of the father as head of the household, wife concerned with motherhood, and children growing up in the faith and traditions of their parents became the embodiment of family.[6] We see the return to this model in the New Testament with Jesus's family.

> When Jesus had finished these parables, he moved on from there. Coming to his hometown, he began teaching the people in their synagogue, and they were amazed. "Where did this man get this wisdom and these miraculous powers?" they asked. "Isn't this the carpenter's son? Isn't his mother's name Mary, and aren't his brothers James, Joseph, Simon and Judas? Aren't all his sisters with us? Where then did this man get all these things?" (Matthew 13:53–56).

In his hometown, Jesus was known by his relationship to his earthly father, mother, and siblings. Today, children are still known by their relationship to family, and most people still consider a family to be at least two people: a married couple with or without children or a single parent with child or children. But the definition of family, as well as the use of the term *head of the household,* has changed. Even the 2010 US Census acknowledged this, describing family as a group of two or more people related by birth, marriage, or adoption and residing together.[7]

The Census Bureau also has recognized a change in what constitutes the head of the household. In 1980, it discontinued the use of the terms *head of household* and *head of family.* Now it uses *householder* and *family householder.* It says, "Recent social changes have resulted in greater sharing of household responsibilities among the adult members and, therefore, have made the term 'head' increasingly inappropriate in the analysis of household and family data."

This realization by the government more than thirty years ago and the rest of society that social changes have resulted in greater sharing of household responsibilities among the adult members is one of the reasons that traditional family roles of the 1950s and 1960s no longer define everyday life, even though about 70 percent of American children live in a home with two parents.

We see this at Journey of Faith when we are adding families to our computerized check-in system. We use a popular web-based database used by many large churches across America. Many of the children in our beach communities and neighboring cities have more than one residence or attend church with only one parent or a grandparent. Another scenario is a child in a two-parent home in which only one of the parents is a Christian who regularly attends church. We have many blended families and families who invite neighborhood children to attend. Registering these various households is sometimes difficult because the database system still tries to have the family registered in the categories of "Head," "Spouse," and "Child."

The decrease in time spent as a family limits the time available to impart a strong sense of shared, godly values to the next generation.

Traditional Roles Have Changed

No matter how many people make up your family, traditional roles have changed as society changed. Back when America was a largely agricultural society, families lived and worked together. As America transitioned away from rural living into city life, opportunities for work outside the home increased. Equity for women in education and in the workplace had a long way to go. In the late 1800s, less than 1 percent of women attended college. That number increased to 7.6 percent in the 1920s. Today, according to the 2010 census, women are just as likely as men to have completed college.

Education for children also changed. Public schools, not the family, became the primary place for education of most children. With the exception of homeschooling families, time spent learning at home decreased, which meant that most of the socialization took place in the community.

This decrease in time spent as a family limits the time available to impart a strong sense of shared, godly values to the next generation.

> He decreed statutes for Jacob and established the law in Israel, which he commanded our forefathers to teach their children, so the next generation would know them, even the children yet to be born, and they in turn would tell their children. Then they would put their trust in God and would not forget his deeds but would keep his commands (Psalm 78:5–7).

We cannot let time become an excuse to fail at developing children and adolescents with a set of biblically based internalized resources from which to make wise decisions when faced with peer pressure or societal fads. We live in a time of social media that give people of all ages, especially teens and young adults, exposure to the society at large with greater ease and a wider reach than ever before. With more children than ever having smartphones, social networking among family and peers is right in the palm of their hands. Have you ever looked on a teen's Facebook profile to see whom they list as their family? Their friends become their siblings. Socially, their identity is now with their peers, rather than with their parents. Once again, our changing society is redefining family.

Protecting the family God gave you, guiding them spiritually and finding healing for yourself and the rest of your kin, depends on stepping out in faith. The following are four steps you can take whether you're a child, parent, grandparent, aunt, uncle, or other member of the "family we got."

Start with a Foundation of Faith

Society will continue to change. Change is inevitable. The changes we have seen in the past decade seem exponential when compared with the changes in the 1950s and 1960s. Look at the amount of dysfunction and abuse we hear about in the media. These reports are usually only for celebrities and politicians. They do not begin to scratch the surface of the increasing chaos in the typical American home. Abuse and addiction is much more prevalent, affecting family members in their teen and childhood years. A child in an abusive home will find it very hard to honor his or her abusing parent. Witnessing or experiencing verbal or physical abuse as a spouse or a child has negative consequences for the entire family. Patterns of abuse affect the child not only in the home, but at school, church, and later on when they have their own relationships. For the spouse, life may seem overwhelming and cause them to question their faith. Depending on who you are or where you live, the embarrassment of admitting that your home is in turmoil may or not be received well by those around you. Do not let your struggles eat away at your soul and rob you of your relationship with your heavenly Father. Confide in someone from your church, such as a Stephen Minister. Find out about support or recovery groups. Seek godly counsel from a trusted friend, relative, or Christian counselor. Knowing you are not alone in your struggles can help you get on the path to restoring your joy.

Families around you are likely experiencing similar disagreements, divorce, difficulties with relatives, or temptations that are seen as commonplace in today's society. So how can we make sure the family we have gives us what we need, rather than what society throws at us? It begins with a foundation of faith—a foundation that is intentionally built on our Christian values, lest we become like the foolish man in the book of Matthew.

"Therefore everyone who hears these words of mine and puts them into practice is like a wise man who built his house on the rock. The rain came down, the streams rose, and the winds blew and beat against that house; yet it did not fall, because it had its foundation on the rock. But everyone who hears these words of mine and does not put them into practice is like a foolish man who built his house on sand. The rain came down, the streams rose, and the winds blew and beat against that house, and it fell with a great crash" (Matthew 7:24–27).

Let's take a look at where you may fall in the institution we call family:

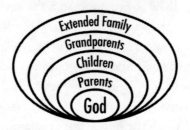

If you are a Christian who is living out your faith, praying daily, worshipping with passion, spending time in the Word, and serving wholeheartedly, then God is at the heart of who you are and the choices you will make on the journey of life. No matter what level of family you fall into, you will be focused on doing God's will and being a beacon of light in your community.

You may be a parent. If you are married, you are like 90 percent of the population.[8] Just because you consider yourself a Christian, don't think that marriage will not require a lifetime of prayer and compromise. Whether you are married, a single parent raising kids on your own, or a single parent sharing custody of children, you have the responsibility for making Christ the center of your home and for showing what it means to be loved unconditionally. This is not done with words alone. How you deal with everyday life has a future effect on your child. Do you pray not only for your family but with your family? Having your family see you reading your Bible at home shows them how important God is to you daily—not just on Sundays. Reading the Bible together is even more powerful.

The Bible is filled with wisdom for us and for our family. We need only ask God with a sincere heart. "If any of you lacks wisdom, he should ask God, who gives generously to all without finding fault, and it will be given to him" (James 1:5). Whether you are a son, a daughter, a parent, a brother, or a sister, you have an important role as a member of your family. Your role is shaped by your relationship with your heavenly Father. Whether you are new in your faith or a longtime believer, God is right there with you, helping you make wise decisions. There is no reason to put all the pressure on yourself when it comes to making decisions that will affect your family. Join a Bible study or take part in a small group. At Journey of Faith, there are small groups for preteens, teens, and adults. There are also classes on Sunday where you can connect with others in your stage of life. God created you to be in relationship. Your family includes not only those living in your home, but your church family as well.

Parents: Make Time for the Simple Things

One of the more difficult things we find in our society is making time for the simple things. With every sport imaginable available to your child, pick one—not three. Sports have great benefits for kids, including hand-eye coordination and how to work together as a team. But try to avoid sports that have games every Sunday, so you can attend church regularly as a family. Take the time to eat together. It does not have to be a five-course meal—but a time to break bread and have fellowship. Fellowship does not only happen at church and in your small group. It should also happen at home with conversations centered on God, where everyone has a chance to participate. Lastly, don't lose your identity in that of your children. One day, they will leave home. Your child will become an adult, and the relationship you once shared will be redefined. With the launch of your child out of your home and into the world, you will find time to rekindle interests of the past, go on a short-term mission trip, or volunteer in your church. Stay connected with your children and continue to pray for them after they have left home.

Children: Love Your Parents

If you are someone's child, you are the next level in our family diagram. In being someone's child, ideally you are blessed to still have one or both parents in your life. They may be a text away or a short drive. They may even be present in your home. So what does God expect of you in the role of the child? " 'Honor your father and your mother, so that you may live long in the land the LORD your God is giving you' " (Exodus 20:12). This Old Testament commandment was not just for those living before the time of Christ. It is repeated six times in the New Testament, validating its relevance in the life of a Christian. And of course, many parents' favorite verse: "Children, obey your parents in everything, for this pleases the Lord" (Colossians 3:20).

Now, that may seem unreasonable, especially if you are a teen. But God gave you the parent or parents you have. Acknowledging the authority of your parents with love and respect pleases God.

Children: Lead Your Friends and Family to God

If you are a child of God, you should recognize that you also have a responsibility to make sure God is present in your family's home. If you actively live out your faith, your family will experience Christ through you. Our youth ministry opens its doors to many teens in the beach cities whose parents do not attend church. You may be one of these teens, or you may have been in this situation at one point in your life.

That was the case in my home. I didn't even know there was a God before a high school friend invited me to church. Let God work through you. Surround yourself with peers who love God as much as you do. Take part in a small group. Grow in knowledge and wisdom and favor with God and men, just as Jesus did. "And Jesus grew in wisdom and stature, and in favor with God and men" (Luke 2:52).

Grandparents: Lead Your Grandchildren

I frequently hear people say they enjoy being grandparents even more than they liked being parents. And as a grandparent, you likely have years of a life lived in faith to pass on to your grandchildren. In the New Testament, Paul noted the faith of Timothy's grandmother: "I have been reminded of your sincere faith, which first lived in your grandmother Lois and in your mother Eunice and, I am persuaded, now lives in you also" (2 Timothy 1:5).

If you are a grandparent, you have lived through the decades of change in America. You have experienced many stages in the journey of life. But some of these changes give you opportunities to connect with your grandchildren who may be farther than a car ride away. Current technology allows you to visit with your grandkids across the country without leaving your home. However, nothing replaces a personal visit. If you live far from your extended family, make every attempt to get together for special events or holidays. Because of your wisdom gained over the years, you have much to offer your family. Faith and godly values should be passed on from generation to generation.

> God also said to Moses, "Say to the Israelites, 'The LORD, the God of your fathers—the God of Abraham, the God of Isaac and the God of Jacob—has sent me to you.' This is my name forever, the name by which I am to be remembered from generation to generation" (Exodus 3:15).

Extended Family: Renew and Revitalize Family Ties

Lastly, we have the extended family. When I think of extended family, I think of the tribes of Israel, camped around the Tabernacle: tent after tent of people connected by a common ancestral line and connected to God. Our extended families, however, are not made of thousands of nomadic tent dwellers living right next to one another. Instead, we live in different cities, states, or countries. Distance need not divide us from our aunts, uncles, and cousins. With each generation, it has become easier to stay in touch and to share stories, photos, and praises. The sibling rivalry that once caused deep divisions has been replaced by shared childhood memories that bring adults and children alike together. It is in times like these when memories, values, and love for God are passed down from generation to generation.

By building on a foundation of faith, taking time for the simple things, loving and honoring our parents, leading our friends and family to God, and strengthening our family ties, we can find healing, harmony, and—on the good days—the peace that God promises us within "the family we got." With the continuing changes in our society, the composition and definitions of family will continue to change. With these inevitable changes, we have one constant—God. "But from everlasting to everlasting the LORD's love is with those who fear him, and his righteousness with their children's children" (Psalm 103:17).

Questions to Ponder and Discuss

1. How did you first learn about God? Was it from your family or someone else in your life? Write down your memory of this event.

2. What qualities or values have you learned from your mom or dad that you find essential in your life today?

3. List the members in your immediate family. Which family member has had the greatest effect on your life and why?

4. How is your vertical relationship with God? Your horizontal relationship with other Christians in your community? If you wanted to change one aspect of either of these relationships, what would you change?

5. Take a moment to pray for your family and to thank God for their influence in your life.

Recommended Reading

10 Building Blocks for a Solid Family by Jim Burns
Spiritual Parenting: An Awakening for Today's Families by Michelle Anthony
The Family: A Christian Perspective on the Contemporary Home by Jack O. Balswick and Judith K. Balswick

The Journey Continues ... With our understanding of the season of family, our study on the journey of life moves forward to examine a couple of possible divergent pathways: singleness (Chapter 3) and marriage (Chapter 4). However, both demand some biblical insight into the relational dance known as dating.

3

Singleness and Dating:
Trusting God with Your Relational Future

Bill Ingram

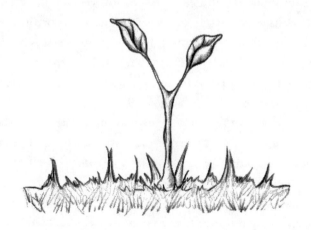

*Whichever calling God has given you,
this season of singleness is a time to grow
as a person and grow in the Lord.*

Being single is not a curse—although many people treat it as such. Mothers openly wonder when their sons and daughters will get married and give them grandchildren. Friends are always trying to fix you up with someone they know "is just perfect" for you. Even churches are not exempt from treating singleness as something that is less than desired. I heard of a church that had a Sunday morning class for young married couples and singles. It was called "Pairs and Spares."

Are You Called to Singleness?

Regardless of how people view singleness, it is not a curse or a sin. It is a calling. This calling may last a season or it may last a lifetime, as it did for Jeremiah the prophet, whom the Lord forbid from marrying (Jeremiah 16:2). Jesus made this very clear in the gospel of Matthew. In Matthew 19:8 Jesus told His disciples that anyone who divorces a spouse for any reason other than marital unfaithfulness and marries another commits adultery. The disciples understood the meaning of Jesus's words and said it would be better not to marry. (I think their response speaks to a culture that did not understand "till death do us part" very well). What follows is profound. Jesus answered, " 'Not everyone can accept this word, but only those to whom it has been given. For some are eunuchs because they were born that way; others were made that way by men; and others have renounced marriage because of the kingdom of heaven. The one who can accept this should accept it' " (Matthew 19:11-12).

The undeniable truth, which Jesus was emphasizing, is that some people are called to be single, and some are called to be married. If you are called to be single, it is so you can devote yourself to God and His service. Paul says, "I would like you to be free from concern. An unmarried man is concerned about the Lord's affairs—how he can please the Lord. ... An unmarried woman or virgin is concerned about the Lord's affairs: Her aim is to be devoted to the Lord in both body and spirit. But a married woman is concerned about the affairs of this world—how she can please her husband" (1 Corinthians 7:32, 34b). Paul is more specific when he says, "I wish that all men were as I am. But each man has his own gift from God; one has this gift, another has that" (1 Corinthians 7:7).

Are You Called to Marriage?

Marriage is instituted and ordained by God but not promised to everyone. Those who are married have not sinned, and those who are single have not sinned (1 Corinthians 7:28). Some of the apostles were married, and others were single. Their marital status was viewed as a calling from God. Singleness may be God's calling on *your* life. If it is, embrace the gift that God has given you and use your time and energy to serve and please Him.

For those who are called to marriage and seeking the person with whom they can spend the rest of their life, the question becomes "How do I find a spouse?" Finding a spouse is not like buying a pair of shoes: we should not try on every pair in the shop to see which one fits best. If we don't like them when we get home, we cannot return them for a model that is newer and fits better.

In the United States, people find their spouses by dating or courting. With everything we do as believers, we need to look to God and His Word to learn what He says about dating. Sadly, there is no chapter in the Bible that spells out the "A-B-Cs" of dating. From what we can tell, Paul did not have a sermon series devoted to dating. There is no record of Jesus teaching a series on finding "Mr. or Miss Right." What the Bible does give us, though, are general principles that we can apply to life in general and dating in particular.

What Does the Bible Say About Dating?

One principle taught in Scripture is that there is no such thing as a "soul mate." Scripture does talk about a "help mate" or a "suitable helper," to quote the New International Version (Genesis 2:20). A "suitable helper" is one who provides what is missing in another. This should not be looked at as demeaning; the word *helper* is used by God in a number of places (Exodus 18:4; Deuteronomy 33:7; 1 Samuel 7:12; Psalm 20:2 and 26:1). There is no person who will fit you perfectly. This idea of finding the one love of your life has been one of the most devastating lies ever conceived. Many marriages have been destroyed by spouses who venture outside marriage to find their "soul mates."

Chemistry ties very closely with an idea of a "soul mate." We have all seen movie scenes of two people locking eyes and gazing at each other across the room. Sparks fly and their hearts beat 100 miles an hour. It is something special, spectacular! We want that magical moment; we desire what the movies are selling. Yet we too often hear, "She is a sweet girl, but we just could not connect" or "He is a really nice guy, but there was no spark." Chemistry is believed to be the missing ingredient.

This feeling we call "chemistry" is created by an actual chemical process. The brain releases chemicals such as phenyl-ethylamine, dopamine, and norepinephrine. These chemicals stimulate the production of adrenaline and give us the feeling that we are in love. Chocolate is full of phenyl-ethylamine, and sometimes our craving for chocolate is our body crying out for this neurotransmitter. According to research, the euphoric state of "feeling in love" typically lasts six months to three years.

Character Should Be the Focus

It is more important to focus on character. Character is not found in the relationship; it resides within a person. A person either has character or doesn't. Within a relationship, character reveals itself in a number of different ways: How does the person treat you? How does the person react to difficulties? Does a person act with integrity when dealing with others? Does the person show respect? Is he or she trustworthy?

Chemistry fades, but good character lasts. I cannot say how much chemistry is needed to have a great relationship, but I do know that you can never have too much character in a relationship.

Dating Is a Process for Finding Our Mates

Dating can be exciting. It can be fun, and it can also be challenging. So when did dating, as we know it, begin? People have some interesting thoughts about dating, and one of them can be found at Answer.Yahoo. com:

Back in the old days, there wasn't the luxury of dating for fun and having a friend of the opposite sex to do things with. Either the parents decided whom their children were going to marry or the man approached the girl's parents to let them know he wanted to marry her. With the parents approval, the man would court the woman, of course being chaperoned by the family. The full intent of dating was to get married and start having a family. Traditions have changed since the old days and now dating has nothing to do with marriage. It's a social tool with no serious intentions behind it.[9]

The best answer that Yahoo can come up with is that dating is "a social tool with no serious intentions behind it." It is just hanging out with a friend and means nothing at all.

Dating is more than having someone of the opposite sex to hang out and do things with. You can do that with friends. Dating is the process we use to determine our life's mates. Proverbs 18:22 says, "He who finds a wife finds what is good and receives favor from the LORD." The word *find* has the meaning "to discover or uncover," and it carries with it the idea of searching to find.

This idea of finding the one love of your life has been one of the most devastating lies ever conceived.

As I have searched the Scripture, there does not appear to be one way that God has specified for us to look for a spouse. Abraham sent his servant to his homeland to find a spouse for Isaac (Genesis 24); Isaac sent Jacob to Paddan Aram to find a wife (Genesis 28), and God told Hosea to marry "an adulterous wife" (Hosea 1). So, how and where do you find a spouse? The answer is by dating.

Developing Spiritual, Emotional, and Financial Wholeness

Before you begin to date, there needs to be wholeness in your life spiritually, emotionally, and financially. Spiritual wholeness means there is a passionate love relationship with Jesus Christ. You have asked Jesus to forgive you of your sins, and you know Jesus as your Savior and Lord. Daily, you seek His wisdom from the study of Scripture and prayer. You are involved with a body of believers who hold you accountable for your actions. You are using your gifts and talents for the kingdom of God. To put it another way, you are a disciple of Jesus Christ. Wholeness in Christ will allow wholeness in another relationship.

Your emotions are the second area of wholeness. You know who you are, and you are comfortable with yourself. You understand your strengths and weaknesses. You are healed from any hurts of past relationships, including damaging family dynamics. It is very difficult to develop a new relationship when you have "baggage" from a past one. Emotional wholeness includes overcoming issues from your childhood. The journey of becoming an emotionally healthy person is vital to any successful relationship.

The third area of wholeness is financial. I know this sounds a little strange, but statistics show that money problems play a large role in couples divorcing. Financial wholeness does not mean that you are rich. It means you have a stable job. Your career path is set, and you are "standing on your own two feet." Your debt is manageable and not growing. As a matter of fact, your debt should be decreasing! Debt is a killer. God calls us to live within our means and to be content with what He has entrusted to us. Learning to budget, spending money based on priorities, knowing when to say yes and no—all this is part of being whole.

It also means that you are no longer living at home. Wholeness means not relying on your parents for support, even for housing. Living on your own is part of the process of leaving your parents and being united with your spouse (Genesis 2:24).

Dating Is Designed to Lead to Marriage

Now that you are ready to date, what do you do? First, *remember that there should be a purpose to dating.* Dating is not a game and should not be treated as such. Dating is designed to lead to marriage. If you have no desire for marriage, or if it is not the right time (for any reason) to be thinking about marriage, don't date. Instead, develop friends of the opposite sex with whom you can do things. If you do this, it is important that you be very clear that this is friendship and not dating.

Also, believe a person who tells you that he or she does not want to get married. "I do not want to get married" is not code for "I have not met the right person yet." Most, if not all, of the time, a person who says this means he or she does not want to get married, and you are just wasting time and energy on a relationship that will go nowhere.

"Must-Haves" and "Would-Likes"

Second, *have a list of "must-haves" and "would-likes."* I am not talking about a written list. But knowing what is important to you in a spouse helps tremendously in the dating process. Knowing and not compromising your must-haves will keep you from investing time and energy in a relationship that will only be dissatisfying and frustrating. A must-have is what it sounds like: a quality, belief, or something else your spouse must have. Good must-haves are always in the areas of beliefs and values, whereas would-likes are in the areas of appearance and hobbies. The more values a couple share, the fewer disagreements they will have and the greater the chance that they will succeed in a marriage.

Only you can determine your must-haves, but I will give you a couple I believe are very important. The first and the most important must-have to look for in a person to date is his or her relationship with Jesus Christ. Any person you date must have turned his or her life over to the Lordship of Jesus Christ.

> Do not be yoked together with unbelievers. For what do righteousness and wickedness have in common? Or what fellowship can light have with darkness? What harmony is there between Christ and Belial? What does a believer have in common with an unbeliever? What agreement is there between the temple of God and idols? For we are the temple of the living God. As God has said: "I will live with them and walk among them, and I will be their God, and they will be my people" (2 Corinthians 6:14–16).

A second important must-have is honesty. This is vital for a healthy, long-term relationship because a person with integrity can be trusted. "Many a man claims to have unfailing love, but a faithful man who can find? The righteous man leads a blameless life; blessed are his children after him" (Proverbs 20:6–7). Jesus taught us that a person who is faithful in the little things will be faithful in the big things. Honest people can be trusted to follow through on their promises and vows.

There may be other must-haves, but the list should not be more than five or six items long. If there are too many, you are setting yourself up for failure. No one is perfect. The would-likes, on the other hand, can be limitless. Just remember not to confuse a would-like with a must-have. A would-like is a preference. It is something you prefer in a person—not something you require in a person. Also, there is nothing inherently right or wrong with a would-like. It can be anything from appearance to hobbies to educational background.

Plan Your Love Life

Planning is an important aspect of life. We plan our careers. We plan where we live, our vacations, and our retirement. But we devote little or no planning at all to our love lives. I think the reason for this is that it is not romantic. A woman wants to be "swept off her feet." The only problem with being swept off your feet is that it hurts when you get dropped on your head. I am amazed by the total lack of planning when it comes to one's dating life. People just kind of let it happen, with no plans. They just go on dating year after year after year and wonder if this is going anywhere, often frustrated that the dating relationship is not moving toward marriage.

A Plan for Dating: Step One

Next have a good plan for dating. Here is one I recommend: three, three, six, and twelve. This is three dates, three months of dating, six months of dating, and twelve months of dating. Everyone gets three dates. The reason is simple: everyone could have a bad date or two. It really takes three dates to get a sense of whether you like this person enough to move to the next level. These dates do not have to be expensive. I recommend just the opposite. They should be light and fun: going out for coffee, having an ice cream together, taking a walk along the beach, playing a round of miniature golf, or having dinner at your favorite local restaurant. The first three dates are a "just getting to know you" time to see if you go to step two. Also, these dates should be interactive: no movies or things that would keep you from talking.

A Plan for Dating: Step Two

Step two is three months of dating. Three months is not dating every day; this is once, maybe twice, a week at most. During this time period, you are examining the character of the person you are dating. Here are some questions to ask yourself: Does this person display godly character? Is this person involved in some kind of ministry? Does this person pray? Does this person pray with me? Praying together is very important because research shows that couples who pray together have a very low divorce rate of about 4 percent.

During this three-month period keep your eyes open for red flags. If you see character traits that aren't what you are looking for, stop dating this person. Among those red flags are visible displays of anger in the person you're dating. The writer of Proverbs says, "An angry man stirs up dissension, and a hot-tempered one commits many sins" (Proverbs 29:22). In another place, he writes, "Do not make friends with a hot-tempered man, do not associate with one easily angered, or you may learn his ways and get yourself ensnared" (Proverbs 22:24–25).

Second, you want to avoid someone who loves money. Paul warns us, "For the love of money is a root of all kinds of evil. Some people, eager for money, have wandered from the faith and pierced themselves with many griefs" (1 Timothy 6:10). If these characteristics are displayed, consider them strong signals to stop dating this person. It is better to be single than to be married to the wrong person.

A Plan for Dating: Step Three

The third stage in the dating process comes after six months of dating. This is a time when the rubber meets the road. This is when true intimacy develops, and you learn more about the other person. You are definitely on the road to marriage. You reveal more of who you are, and your dating partner reveals more of who he or she is.

By now, the two of you have gone through at least two seasons together, and ideally shared a holiday or two. It is at this time that you might want to take a trip together. Here are the boundaries of traveling when not married. Travel with another couple and have separate rooms. This speaks volumes to your commitment to Christ and is a witness to those outside the church. Traveling together accomplishes two things. First, it adds a little stress to the relationship so you can see how the other person responds. A little pressure is good for a relationship. It helps build unity. Second, a person cannot hide who he or she is when traveling. It is hard to hide your real self when under pressure. If during this six-month period you see a characteristic or characteristics that are troubling, a decision must be made. You must ask yourself, "Can I live with this forever?" If the answer is no, it may be time to stop dating this person. Remember, it is better to be single than to be married to the wrong person.

A Plan for Dating: The Fourth and Final Step

The fourth and final stage in the process comes at twelve months. At this point in the relationship, you should be getting engaged. You have been through the four seasons. You know what to expect; you know how your potential mate is going to react. You should be sure that this is the person you want to marry. If you are not sure by now, it is time to move on.

Remaining Pure

During the stages of dating, keeping yourself pure is of vital importance. Paul says the following:

> It is God's will that you should be sanctified: that you should avoid sexual immorality; that each of you should learn to control his own body in a way that is holy and honorable, not in passionate lust like the heathen, who do not know God; and that in this matter no one should wrong his brother or take advantage of him. The Lord will punish men for all such sins, as we have already told you and warned you. For God did not call us to be impure, but to live a holy life. Therefore, he who

rejects this instruction does not reject man but God, who gives you his Holy Spirit (1 Thessalonians 4:3–8).

Let me speak very clearly here: God expects us to remain pure until we get married. We should not play games! Purity is not refraining from one specific act while participating in another. You are not being pure just because you do not have marital relationships. Paul put it this way:

> Flee from sexual immorality. All other sins a man commits are outside his body, but he who sins sexually sins against his own body. Do you not know that your body is a temple of the Holy Spirit, who is in you, whom you have received from God? You are not your own; you were bought at a price. Therefore honor God with your body (1 Corinthians 6:18–20).

Science has finally caught up with Scripture on this point. Paul warned us to flee sexual immorality because when we participate in God's design for intimacy, we become one with someone else. Science tells us that a bonding occurs. Purity starts with our minds. Jesus said the following:

> "You have heard that it was said, 'Do not commit adultery.' But I tell you that anyone who looks at a woman lustfully has already committed adultery with her in his heart. If your right eye causes you to sin, gouge it out and throw it away. It is better for you to lose one part of your body than for your whole body to be thrown into hell. And if your right hand causes you to sin, cut it off and throw it away. It is better for you to lose one part of your body than for your whole body to go into hell" (Matthew 5:27–30).

Thoughts lead to actions! Keeping your thoughts pure is one way to keep you from sinning in this area. Purity involves your mind as well as your body! The best way to manage physical involvement is to set strong, definite boundaries before anything happens. These boundaries need to be agreed upon ahead of time. Yes, this takes away being "caught up in the moment," but that is the point. When self-control is practiced, we honor God with our bodies.

With planning and prayer, being single and dating can be a great time in the journey to marriage and family. Or being single can be your calling to fully devote yourself to God and other aspects of the journey of life. Whichever calling God has given you, this season of singleness is a time to grow as a person and grow in the Lord. It is a great time to develop friendships and serve God without distractions. It is a blessing—not a curse.

Questions to Ponder and Discuss

1. How do you know if God has called you to a life of singleness? What are the greatest joys in this calling? What are some of the challenges to this calling? How can God receive glory in both?

2. What are appropriate and inappropriate physical expressions of affection before marriage? How does Scripture address this subject? In what ways can physical intimacy before marriage negatively affect your judgment about a potential spouse or the relationship?

3. How do you know when to stop dating someone? What are the characteristics being displayed during dating that are not conducive to a good marriage?

4. Why do people continue to date the wrong person? How can this cycle be broken? What does the Bible say about seeking God's will and godly counsel when making these decisions? What should we say or not say to friends or family members who we believe are dating the wrong person?

5. Should parents give their blessing before a couple is engaged? Does this change with age? Why or why not? How does the biblical command to "honor your father and mother" come into play?

Recommended Reading

Boundaries in Dating: Making Dating Work by Henry Cloud and John
    Townsend
Finding the Love of Your Life by Neil Clark Warren
Marriable, Taking the Desperate Out of Dating by Hayley DeMaraco and
    Michael DiMarco

The Journey Continues ... As we move beyond the season of dating, many hope and anticipate a new season of marriage. Where we have already examined the "family we got," we now take a look at the "family we choose." We also remind you that this is one of the most important choices you will ever make because you invite someone else to join you on your lifelong journey. Turn the pages carefully, looking for biblical insights for the season of marriage.

4

Marriage:
Choosing God's Best
with the One You Love

Jason Cusick

*For those who have chosen marriage and family,
it is part of that radical call of Jesus.*

As we have already learned, there are many ways to define *family.* There are traditional families, blended families, adoptive families, "alternative" families, and a wide variety of other kinds of families. Our culture is fighting over the definitions because "family" means so much to us. Marriage is another subject of heated debate. What does the Bible say about marriage and family? What are the essentials we need to know? How can we have the kind of marriages and families that God desires?

Choosing Your Family

Jill and Todd reached a crossroads in their relationship. Because of a variety of factors, including work, family, money, and their individual spiritual lives, they realized their marriage wasn't what it could be. Jill's friends blamed Todd. Todd's friends told him he deserved to be happy. They didn't know what to do. They made a courageous first step. They took a look at themselves and their marriage. They made a plan to have a better marriage than they'd been having. They made a choice.

You must choose your family. Having a strong marriage is a choice. This choice happens daily, often with small decisions or with a choice about how you are going to talk with, think about, or behave toward your spouse. This choice also happens at a deep heart level. "Am I willing to do whatever it takes to be the wife or husband I am supposed to be?"

Whom Do You Imitate?

Have you noticed that the more time you spend with a person, the more you become like them? The Bible says, " 'Bad company corrupts good character' " (1 Corinthians 15:33). The people we spend the most time with are most likely to shape our thinking, emotions, and behaviors. Our family and friends can powerfully influence us. But before you start thinking about which of your family members and friends are hurting or helping, take a moment to think about yourself. Whom do *you* imitate?

A psychologist recently told me that when she meets with couples for marriage counseling, it is not difficult to discover how the problems in the relationship have formed. After a few sessions of some background information, hidden "scripts" and deeply ingrained habits begin to show their origins. "He is imitating the angry and nonverbal behaviors his father modeled." Or "she is modeling the critical, reactive actions her mother taught her." Most of the time, the imitation is not intentional. It just happens. When we spend a lot of time around a person, we slowly begin to act like that person.

The apostle Paul noticed all kinds of unhealthy and sinful behavior in his church—harsh words, loneliness, anger, silent treatments, mistrust, selfishness, sexual sin, and infidelity. His advice to them was profoundly simple: "Be imitators of God" (Ephesians 5:1a).

The foundation of a great marriage and family is found in those we imitate. What does imitating God look like? It doesn't mean using *thee* and *thou* in your sentences or dressing in long robes and finding friends named Adam to touch fingers with. In fact, that form of imitation is sure to put you in something other than a great marriage! Paul's idea of imitation is much more practical. He recommends the following in Ephesians:

> Stop bickering and talking bad about your partner to other people (4:31).
> Be gentle and don't be mean (4:32).
> Put up with people's mistakes like God puts up with yours (4:32).
> Deal with your sexual sins and sexual problems (5:3).
> Don't keep wanting things other people have (5:3).
> Shut your potty mouth and stop making jokes at the expense of others (5:4).
> Be thankful for what God has given you (5:4).
> Think each day about how you can live for God (5:15).
> Stop letting alcohol control you; give that privilege to God's Spirit (5:18).
> Learn the encouraging words in your Bible and quote them often (5:19).

How do you live up to these ten examples? The most difficult part of imitating God is coming to the point of realizing that we need to—or else. Some couples discover this too late. Infidelity, neglect, deep resentments, or abuse cause a spouse to leave. But things don't have to be this bad for us to want to have the kind of marriage God wants. We should always be improving, growing, and learning more about the amazing things He wants to do in our marriages.

Baptizing Your Marriage

My wife and I have yearly themes in our marriage. Every year we sense what God wants to do in our relationship. One year it was "having the courage to be brutally honest." Another year was "the year of financial changes." This year is something very different. It is very easy to let years go by without doing anything to improve our relationships. Many couples have fallen asleep on the job. Paul's message is clear: " 'Wake up, O sleeper, rise from the dead, and Christ will shine on you' " (Ephesians 5:14).

Many Bible scholars believe these were the words from an ancient Christian baptismal hymn. Can you imagine people getting baptized and the congregation singing these words? It's like the person being baptized saying, "I want my life to be different. I want to put the old way of doing things behind me and let Jesus's love shine through me." The congregation would reply in song: "Then wake up and live a new life. That's what Jesus wants too!"

I had the pleasure of baptizing a man who had come to Christ after a long journey of questions. His wife was a Christian already. When talking about getting baptized, he asked if his wife could be beside him in the water. He said, "This is like a new start to our marriage." I believe God wants to give us new starts continually. Each day has the possibility for a new beginning.

This story may be a bit tough for those who are in a "spiritually mixed" marriage. Having a spiritual awakening and a new spiritual beginning is different when marriage partners don't share the same spiritual beliefs. "Awakenings" are different in these marriages. Sensitivity, patience, and humble communication can lead to new beginnings, even when spiritual unity is not there. Whether your marriage has a strong foundation in Christ or not, God desires new beginnings for your marriage, which begin as we "wake up."

Who Is Your Boss?

When we were teaching our son about responsibility and obedience, we told him, "Everyone has a boss. No matter what age, job, or time in your life, you will always have a boss. The best thing you can do is figure out who that is."

Then I asked, "Who is your boss?"

"Mom," he replied.

"Who's Mom's boss?" I asked.

He replied, "You, Dad." (I paused and looked over my shoulder as all my traditional and patriarchal views came bubbling to the surface.)

"Okay," I said. "Who's my boss?"

He stopped and thought for moment. "God," he said and then quickly added, "Wait a minute, God is the boss of all of us!"

Unlike the "household codes" of the ancient world, the apostle Paul presented a radical view of marriage and family for Christians. He declared, "God is the boss of us all!" What this means is that although there are differences in responsibilities and roles in a marriage, Christian husbands and wives are to "submit to one another" (Ephesians 5:21). In the ancient world, women were inferior. Paul reminded people of what God had revealed in Scripture from the beginning: both men and women have equal value, standing, and power from God. This was revolutionary to the original readers. It made them rethink how many of their views were cultural rather than biblical. We have this problem today. Many Americans consider the "traditional American family" to be equal to the "biblical family." Variables such as family size, relationship to extended family, values, dual-income earners, and division of domestic duties are often culturally defined.

There are only a few things about marriage that are clearly defined. A person should seek out a like-minded believer to marry (2 Corinthians 6:14–16). God wants people to be married to someone of the opposite sex (Genesis 2:21–25, 1 Corinthians 6:9–11). Husbands and wives should be faithful to each other and fight to stay together for life (Matthew 19:3–6). In the event of a painful separation or divorce, God's Word should be followed with the support and guidance of a trusted spiritual community (Matthew 19:8, 1 Corinthians 7:12–16). There are also specific instructions for wives and husbands.

Do You Know How to "Yield"?

The Bible instructs wives to "submit" to their husbands (Ephesians 5:22–24). Much ink has been spilled on this subject. Centuries of abuse, misuse, and ego have complicated its application. There is no secret or profoundly insightful way to translate the word from its Greek original. *Hupotassoe* means "submit, yield oneself to." We know that it does *not* mean "to obey." Paul uses a different word in relationship to children and parents (Ephesians 6:1). So what does "submission" look like? Gary Thomas, author of *Sacred Influence,* says, "Women are not told to sit passively on the sidelines and cheer for their husbands as the men run the show. On the contrary, from the very beginning women share God's command for humans to rule, subdue, and manage this earth. They are co-regents."[10]

Instead of explaining what submission is, Paul gives a picture. He says that wives should submit to their husbands like the church submits to Christ. I've been a part of churches long enough to see what happens when the church doesn't submit to Christ. Christians have a tendency to get way ahead of themselves, not talk to God about what's going on, make all kinds of decisions on their own, and behave like they are accountable to no one. The opposite is just as damaging: sitting idly and waiting for specific instructions, and then obeying out of fear of being struck down from heaven. Some marriages operate at these extremes: wives aggressively planning and executing their personal desires of what they think would be best without cooperating with their husbands or fearfully and dutifully doing whatever their husbands say out of a lack of confidence.

When a wife "yields to" her husband as she would to Christ, she is respecting who God made—*and is making*—her husband to be. A wife makes it a priority to cooperate with her husband and not dominate him or make him unnecessary by taking his role in the marriage and family. Wives "yield" when they discover their strengths, gifts, and power from God and use it in partnership with their husbands—not as independent agents. It's about valuing him for who he is and what God is doing in and through him, like how we are to value each part of the body (1 Corinthians 12:14–27). We yield when we trust that God is working in and through someone very different from ourselves.

Who (or What) Do You Love?

Men are built to love. We have strong passions and desires. We like to take care of things, build things, and grow things. When men love, they love deeply. Attend a local car rally or visit a guy's "man cave" and you can see what happens when men have a passion. When men choose to love something, they go all out. Unfortunately, things and people are not the same. Loving relationships are sometimes difficult for men.

Culture has contributed to this. Men are the comic relief in most television shows. They are seen as the bumbling fools of the family. In their early years, men hear unbiblical messages about manhood, such as "men never cry" or "men never show weakness." In the last twenty years, men have been encouraged to "get in touch with their feminine side." As they have experimented with trying to be more of what women want, they've become wimps. Men have fallen into the same trap women have been trying to climb out of—trying to be something that somebody else wants them to be. What is a man to do?!

The Bible calls a husband to love his wife (Ephesians 5:25). Notice that the verse does not call him to "lead" his wife. Husbands *do* need to step up into leadership. They need to ask God for direction, courage, strength, and integrity for their families. They should not be passive or slip into culturally defined stereotypes. Wives want their husbands to "lead," but what do they mean when they say this?

> *The ultimate goal of marriage is for a man and a woman to become so connected in their commitment to God and each other that they each consider their spouse part of their own body.*

This passage specifically instructs them to "love." A husband must be committed to making sacrifices, which will exalt, affirm, and protect his wife. When a husband loves his wife, he devotes time, energy, and commitment to her. He considers her part of himself and rightly takes care of her. It is not about leading; it is about loving! It is what Christ loving us looks like (Ephesians 5:25–27). The image of marriage that Paul gives is not a business model of leader and subordinate but an organic image of head and body: two parts working together as one. In their book, *Just How Married Do You Want to Be?*, Jim and Sarah Sumner write the following:

> By God's design, the husband is inclined to make choices for himself that accord with his own preferences. So when a husband starts to

realize that his wife's preferences are part of his identity as a husband, he begins to understand that in loving her, he is loving himself.[11]

When husbands love their wives, amazing things happen. When they do this, husbands can partner with their wives in God's gracious gift of life (1 Peter 3:7). What is competing for your love?

With Whom Are You Intimate?

The apostle Paul ends his instructions on marriage with a word about "body loving" (Ephesians 5:28–33). He quotes Genesis 2:24: "For this reason a man will leave his father and mother and be united to his wife, and they will become one flesh." The ultimate goal of marriage is for a man and a woman to become so connected in their commitment to God and each other that they each consider their spouse part of their own body. In our age of brokenness, many would take issue with Paul's words, "no one ever hated his own body." Christians and non-Christians struggle with problems such as cutting, sexual addiction, gluttony, eating disorders, poor body image, and self-hatred. These are most damaging to marriages because they compromise biblical intimacy.

People who do not have biblical self-images cannot bring themselves fully to their spouses. A biblical self-image is when one sees oneself as a masterpiece and created in the image of God but flawed and imperfect (Ephesians 2:1–10). Couples struggle when their self-image emphasizes one part of the above description more than the other—being shamefully insecure or pridefully selfish.

Real connection and intimacy happen when a husband and wife can bring their gifted but broken selves to each other. Sex is the fullest expression of this kind of connection. Marriages are not great because of great sex. Great sex comes from a great marriage. Sadly, many couples are struggling with their sexual intimacy. Recent research reveals that sexless marriages are more common (and more damaging) than we think.[12] The Bible does say that there are times when a couple may make a decision to refrain from sex for some greater purpose, but this should be temporary, mutually agreed on, and spiritually guarded (1 Corinthians 7:3–5). For today's couples, busy schedules, poor communication, stress, depression, pornography, and other forms of sexual brokenness from the past can all contribute to a couple's lack of intimacy. "Becoming one" in spirit and body is God's desire for husbands and wives. It is something we must "wake up" to and pursue.

Who Is on Your Side?

Marriage can be a battle. Many couples battle against each other and fail to recognize that they are allowing Satan to destroy their marriage. After Paul's instructions to husbands, wives, children, and others, he turns his attention to the subject of "spiritual warfare" (Ephesians 6:10–18). He dramatically writes, "For our struggle is not against flesh and blood, but against the rulers, against the authorities, against the powers of this dark world and against the spiritual forces of evil in the heavenly realms" (Ephesians 6:12).

Before we let our home-front battles get the best of us, we need to be aware that the Enemy enjoys pitting us against one another. It can happen very subtly—a spouse's words are taken the wrong way, a sinful thought slips out during an argument, or something is brought up from the past. It can also be very direct: a wife gives into temptation with a coworker or a husband decides to release his anger and becomes violent. These spiritual battles are often the sign of invisible wars of the heart.

Marriages are successful and strong when there is a good support team in place. This begins with each person submitting to God and each other, but one's friends are vitally important. Florence Isaacs in *Toxic Friends, True Friends,* writes the following:

> Friends can lighten things up and take some of the heat off marriage, so you don't feel overburdened in meeting all of your partner's needs ... however, certain friendships are negative influences that weaken bonds with your spouse. It's important to recognize friendships that enrich your marriage—and be aware of those that can divide.[13]

The epic love poem of the Bible, The Song of Songs (Solomon), tells the story of a couple deeply in love. They are passionate and spiritual, but their relationship is not without its struggles. The poem contains alternating words from the man, the woman, and a group of people called "the chorus." In ancient theater, the chorus was a group of people on stage who narrated the story, presented conflict, or encouraged the characters toward a happy ending.

Every marriage needs a "good chorus" of friends. These are the people who can hear the struggles but will always challenge a husband and wife to follow God and become better marriage partners. A "good chorus" will help confront sin as well as bind and care for wounds. Wives need to have strong godly female friends who will encourage them to love their husbands, avoid sin, and be kind (Titus 2:3–5). Husbands need strong Christian male friends to encourage them to be self-controlled in their words, actions, and relationships (Titus 2:6). There are times when friendships must end or change because they cannot or will not support the marriage. These can be painful decisions. When husbands and wives have a "good chorus" of friends, they are making a choice to protect their marriage from attack and ensure strength, wisdom, and support in challenging times (Proverbs 24:6). Who is in your "good chorus"?

Choosing a Strong Marriage

Having a strong marriage is indeed a choice based on the big decisions about faith, family, and the future as well as the small day-to-day determinations of how we treat one another. Amid the many choices we face, choosing to have a strong and faithful marriage is becoming increasingly "countercultural." This is great news for Christians, because following Jesus has always been "countercultural." This kind of marriage is for those who are not content to settle, compromise, or give in to what everyone else is doing. Christians are those who are willing to sacrifice themselves for something great and powerful and God ordained. They are committed to true love—the kind of love that is possible when God is at the center of their lives. For those who have chosen marriage and family, it is part of that radical call of Jesus.

All-powerful and loving God, you desire marriage to be a picture of your loving faithfulness to us and our commitment to you. Help our marriages, and the marriages of those we know, better reflect this reality of our relationship with you. Help us have hearts that yield, lead, love, and fight for what you want. Break us, mold us, and open us to the guidance of others as we choose to follow your leading for the best marriage you have to offer us. In Jesus's name, amen.

Questions to Ponder and Discuss

1. Who are the people who have most influenced you in your life? Describe a positive influence and a negative influence. How much influence do God and the Bible have on your thinking, feelings, and behaviors in your marriage? Name one way in which you can allow God to have more influence in your life.

2. On a scale of 1 to 5, how submissive do you consider yourself? In what ways do you see the strength and value of your role as a wife? In what ways are you dissatisfied? What is that dissatisfaction a response to: God's order for marriage in His Word? Your life stage? The behavior of your partner? Other factors? What is God calling you to do regardless of the circumstances?

3. Who (or what) is most likely to compete for the love of your partner? Be specific. How could you begin to shift your love back to your spouse? How does the idea of "loving" versus "leading" change the way you relate to your wife? Name one sacrifice you can begin making to improve the way in which you love your wife.

4. Why is it difficult for Christians to talk about sex and intimacy? Do you think this topic is easier to discuss now than in the past? Are there some areas of sexual brokenness listed in this chapter that you need to address? Be specific.

5. Who is part of your "chorus" of friends? Are there people in your life who are not supportive of (or even antagonistic toward) your marriage? What level of involvement or influence do they have? From whom do you get support, direction, guidance, and correction? Who helps you shed your biases?

Recommended Reading

Sacred Marriage by Gary Thomas
Surviving a Spiritual Mismatch by Lee Strobel and Leslie Strobel
Before a Bad Goodbye: How to Turn Your Marriage Around by Tim Clinton

The Journey Continues ... We have learned that God values life, and you do not live your life in isolation: you are born into a family. What is amazing is that one day God may bring you into a marriage relationship where His will includes you and your spouse having a baby to raise and guide through his or her initial journey of life. For most parents, this can be overwhelming. So we have included the following chapter, written by two gifted youth pastors, to give you research and insight into the season of parenting and beyond.

5

Parenting:
Moving Your Children
Toward Spiritual Development

Michelle Browne / Matt Johnston

*If you are strategic in your parenting
and make a purposeful effort to live out
your faith, your children will be more likely
to live for God for a lifetime.*

By now, you are probably familiar with the story of a young man who grew up in a small town in the middle of nowhere. Having grown up without both his parents, he lived in the home of his aunt and uncle. He had plenty of friends, but he felt trapped. His uncle was a farmer and expected him to one day take over the family business. His aunt, a sweet and understanding woman, loved him. But she could see his desire to move away and start his own life somewhere else had consumed him. Then tragedy struck. His aunt and uncle were viciously murdered, and this young man was alone again. However, the tenacity of the human spirit is a powerful force. This young man went on to find his long-lost twin sister. With the help of friends, he blew up the most destructive weapon known to humankind—the DeathStar—and saved the galaxy. As one thinks of unbelievable characters, like the fictional Luke Skywalker of "Star Wars" fame, it is easy to understand why epic movies and stories like his have captured the love and admiration of generations. These movies tell great stories!

Writing Remarkable Stories

So how do great stories and parenting relate to each other? Simply put, one of the most important things you can do in raising your children is to challenge them to *write remarkable stories with their lives*! Kids need to know that God has given them an amazing story that He wants each of them to live out, and parents can help them see that vision and accomplish His specific plan. Jesus said in John 10:10, " 'The thief comes only to steal and kill and destroy; I have come that they may have life, and have it to the full.' " This is the kind of life that God intends for each child!

If you want to help your children write extraordinary stories with their lives, it's worth asking what makes a great story. A great story requires a good character who wants something and must overcome conflict to get it.[14] But how does that apply to raising children? That question will be addressed in this chapter.

Spiritual Development Is the First Priority

What should you want for your children? According to Dr. James Dobson in his book *Bringing Up Boys,* the number one priority of parenting should be the spiritual development of children, especially at an early age.[15] Deuteronomy 6:6–9 says,

> These commandments that I give you today are to be on your hearts. Impress them on your children. Talk about them when you sit at home and when you walk along the road, when you lie down and when you get up. Tie them as symbols on your hands and bind them on your foreheads. Write them on the doorframes of your houses and on your gates.

These verses underscore the fact that a child's spiritual development happens every day, all day long. Talking about spiritual issues should be a normal, daily part of the family's routine.

In addition, children should be taught the difference between a "rules-based religion" and a "relationship-based faith." Too often, children think they are spiritual and godly if they obey the "rules" of their faith. But in many instances, their hearts are far from God. A rules-based religion produces an empty and legalistic view of God and faith. Students should be taught that true Christianity is about a sincere love and passion for God and that living a life of obedience and surrender flows out of that love.

The late philosopher Dr. Francis Schaeffer wrote, "The dilemma of modern man is simple: He does not know why man has any meaning … This is the damnation of our generation, the heart of modern man's problem."[16] Even though this quote was written almost three decades ago, it is even more relevant to today's children and teenagers. Several years ago, Word Publishing put together focus groups in various cities regarding this topic. Their findings were enlightening. They found that the most common concern of the younger generation was the absence of meaning in life. These kids, many of them Christians, were confused about the purpose of their lives.[17]

If students are educated on what true Christianity entails and about their God-given purpose, then the chances of them writing an amazing story with their lives will be exponentially greater. From a humble youth pastor perspective, there are three very applicable and practical steps that will aid in a student's spiritual development, and they are listed below.

Step One: Life-Changing Prayer

Although it may sound cliché, the *most* important contribution you can make to your children's spiritual development is prayer. The importance of *daily* prayer cannot be overstated. In John 6:44, Jesus says, " 'No one can come to me unless the Father who sent me draws him, and I will raise him up at the last day.' " Prayer is a life-changing, powerful force in a child's life, and it is the primary agent by which God draws people to Himself.

Whether it is praying in a prayer group, praying for each child out loud before bed, or praying in the car before school, these times of prayer can have a powerful effect on a child's spiritual development. First Thessalonians 5:16–18 says, "Be joyful always; pray continually; give thanks in all circumstances, for this is God's will for you in Christ Jesus." Praying for and praising God for your children is an important aspect of God's will for your life.

Step Two: Teaching a Child to Step Out in Faith

Teaching your children to step out in faith is another important lesson. Young people today are yearning for so much more than the mediocre, blasé religion of the past. They are seeking adventure, danger, and excitement— and a life lived out for Jesus Christ is exactly that. Thus, putting students in uncomfortable, challenging situations is a *must*. In his book *Wild at Heart* John Eldredge says, "Desire reveals design, and design reveals destiny." Students need to be challenged to "get out of the boat" and put their faith into action. When students do this, their faith becomes real, authentic, and deeply personal.

But with taking risks comes fear—fear of rejection, fear of failure, and fear of abandonment. That is why you need to remind your children that they are unconditionally loved. David Popenoe, professor of sociology at Rutgers University and co-chair of the Council of Families in America, wrote, "Children develop best when they are provided the opportunity to have warm, intimate, continuous, and enduring relationships with both their fathers and their mothers."[18] Even the parable of the prodigal son, found in Luke, echoes this concept beautifully. " 'So he got up and went to his father. But while he was still a long way off, his father saw him and was filled with compassion for him; he ran to his son, threw his arms around him and kissed him' " (Luke 15:20). The power of unconditional love cannot be underestimated, and it helps provide the framework in which your children will feel safe to live and step out in faith.

Just as each child is unique and different, so too they differ in how they experience and value love. In his book *The Five Love Languages of Teenagers* Gary Chapman says that every teenager values and views love in five different ways: words of affirmation, physical touch, quality time, acts of service, and gifts.[19] Understanding these concepts will help you express love to your children and grow closer.

Step Three: Being a Role Model

> Being a role model is the most powerful form of educating. Youngsters need good models more than they need critics. It's one of a parent's greatest responsibilities and opportunities. The person you are is the person your child will become.
> —Legendary Coach and Author John Wooden[20]

Jesus Himself knew the importance of role modeling. After He had washed His disciples' feet, He said, " 'I have set you an example that you should do as I have done for you' " (John 13:15). What Jesus taught about service is also true about parenting. If you want your kids to pray fervently, then you need to pray fervently. If you want your children to love God passionately, then you need to love God passionately. If you want your kids to make wise choices, then you need to do the same. Children are incredibly sensitive and astute. They have an uncanny ability to distinguish between adults who only talk a good game and those who play the game by the rules they preach.

In addition, George Barna, a renowned Christian researcher and marketing expert, found that a parent's behavior and parenting style is the number one spiritual influence in a child's life. "Parenting by default and trial-and-error parenting are both approaches that enable parents to raise their children without the effort of defining their life," Barna explained:

> Revolutionary parenting, which is based on one's faith in God, makes parenting a life priority. Those who engage in revolutionary parenting

define success as intentionally facilitating faith-based transformation in the lives of their children, rather than simply accepting the aging and survival of the child as a satisfactory result.[21]

If you are strategic in your parenting and make a purposeful effort to live out your faith, your children will be more likely to live for God for a lifetime.

Although these three aspects—prayer, stepping out in faith, and role modeling—are excellent springboards for developing a child's faith, they do not guarantee that a child will grow up and live for God. Each child must make his or her own choice about his or her faith. What God does require is that you, as a parent, love, discipline, and instruct your children about His will. But the ultimate decision belongs to each child.

If you want your children to tell extraordinary stories with their lives, then you will want them to have vibrant, thriving relationships with the Creator of the universe. However, in order to live that out, we must look at the second part of the definition for a great story, which says that in addition to wanting something, the good character must *overcome conflict* to get it. Five main sources of conflict must be overcome to allow students to live what we call "sold-out" lives for Jesus Christ.

Source of Conflict 1: Growing Up Too Fast

No one can deny that kids are growing up much faster these days than in the past. With growth spurts, especially around puberty, come an onslaught of emotional and physical changes. As children's brains develop, neural connectors release hormones that trigger intense emotions. By acknowledging these emotions, you can assure your children that what they are experiencing is normal, and they are not "crazy."

As teens' brains change and evolve, so do their bodies, and these changes are taking place faster than ever before. A few generations ago, teens typically experienced puberty between the ages of thirteen and sixteen. Now, the average age range is nine through twelve![22]

Kay Hymowitz, contributor of the *Wall Street Journal*, wrote an article titled "Kids Today Grow Up Way Too Fast." She cited five reasons for this alarming trend. One was a lack of parental supervision. Whether by choice or necessity, teens today are left alone much more often than they were in the past. This lack of parental oversight has led to less accountability and more experimentation. Another reason kids are growing up faster than before is what the *Wall Street Journal* describes as "a sexualized and glitzy media-driven marketplace." If parents and mentors do not educate their children about purpose and perspective on life, the media culture will! (Just observe the popularity of the reality television shows such as *Jersey Shore* and *16 and Pregnant* on MTV.)

Third, with the increase in electronic communication, teens are feeling more isolated than ever. They get their validation and education in the form of digital messaging, thus adding more validity to the already glamorized media marketplace. Fourth, since many of their peers find themselves in similar situations, a strong sense of community is formed with their attitudes, principles, and actions being shaped by media-based resources and programming instead of parental advice or insight. Add to that the fifth dimension of premature physical development, and it can create a recipe for disaster if parents are not informing or educating their children.[23]

If students are educated on what true Christianity entails and about their God-given purpose, then the chances of them writing an amazing story with their lives will be exponentially greater.

By being supportive and understanding, you can be a tremendous help to your children as they negotiate the difficulties of growing up emotionally and physically and make the transition from childhood to adulthood.

Source of Conflict 2: Technology/Media

Another source of conflict that teens must wrestle with is the ever-increasing presence of technology. Technology in and of itself is amoral. Teens are given the opportunity to use technology in both positive and negative ways. They can take a strong stand for Christ, witness to their friends, and even debate the key issues of faith with classmates and people all over the world. In addition, teens are able to stay more connected with the use of technology, adding to their safety. Technology offers other advantages as well, like giving quieter kids a voice and allowing parents to listen in through social media sites, for example.[24]

But there is also a dark side. Cyber bullying, child predation, and cyber stalking are all dangers associated with the use of electronic communication. No matter what form of technology you permit, you should establish standards for its use and be sure to enforce those standards through monitoring and supervision. More than 85 percent of teenagers have access to the Internet through various forms of technology, but only one-quarter of them have rules on how to use it.[25] *Trust, but verify—always*!

Because of the proliferation of technology in our world, marketers and media outlets are finding more and more ways to get their messages out to the masses. Media has life-shaping power. For instance, a sixteen-year-old student may say when confronted about certain types of behavior, "It's just what you do when you're in high school. It's not a big deal. ... It's just like in the movies." Teens see portrayals of how "it's supposed to be" and desperately aspire to emulate unhealthy activities.

Another key point to keep in mind is that these behaviors and worldviews are not adopted instantaneously. They have been incrementally communicated through repeated exposure to media portrayals and messages. Young people are very vulnerable to media's life-shaping power. And, with the emerging generation of teenagers spending greater amounts of time with a growing number of media outlets, media's power has greatly increased.[26]

MEDIA SAYS ... (The Lie)	GOD SAYS ... (The Truth)
To be worthwhile, you must be beautiful.	I care about who you are, not what you look like. (1 Peter 3:3–4)
Avoid pain and pursue pleasure at all costs.	Expect suffering and exercise perseverance. (Romans 5:3–4)
Sex is a recreational pursuit. There are no consequences, and everybody does it.	I've given you the gift of sexuality for the purpose of procreation, intimacy, and expressing oneness in marriage. (1 Corinthians 7:4)
Violence is an acceptable way to deal with your problems.	Turn the other cheek and love your enemies. (Matthew 5:38–42)

In the real world, it's okay to use anyone for any purpose.	Treat people with dignity, love your neighbor and sacrifice your own rights for the rights of others. (Deuteronomy 15:7–11)
Money brings happiness, and you should grab and hold onto all the stuff you can.	Seek first my kingdom and don't worry about the things that moth and rust so easily destroy. (Matthew 6:19-21)

As Christians, we can adopt one of two different philosophies as it pertains to our children's use of media outlets around them: the "monk" or the "miner." The monk places extremely strict limits on the types of entertainment programs allowed in the home. The monk rejects all forms of secular movies, music, and entertainment. The miner acknowledges that certain content must be rejected by Christians but that some secular entertainment has value. This philosophy holds that Christians must be discerning enough to teach kids the difference between entertainment that is biblically acceptable and that which is not. Obviously, you must choose which approach is right for your family. There are advantages and disadvantages to both.

Source of Conflict 3: A Hyper-Sexualized Society

Again, "the media" is not the enemy. But when left unchecked, it can harm a child's worldview by delivering a hyper-sexualized message. The American Academy of Pediatrics' 2001 policy statement "Sexuality, Contraception, and the Media" said this: "The average young viewer is exposed to more than 14,000 sexual references each year, yet only a handful provide an accurate portrayal of responsible sexual behavior or accurate information about birth control, abstinence, or the risks of pregnancy and sexually transmitted disease."[27]

Students are constantly bombarded with images of sex and sexuality, yet the statistics are surprising. Between 1995 and 2002, the percentage of teens who had ever had sex declined from 49 percent to 46 percent among females and from 55 percent to 46 percent among males. And during that time, only 46 percent of all fifteen- to nineteen-year-olds in the United States claimed to have had sex.[28] Yet our hyper-sexualized society paints a totally different picture. The idea that "everyone's doing it" is clearly a lie. (Some of the common reasons for the decline in sexual activity include future college plans and health-related issues, such as sexually transmitted diseases and fear of pregnancy. Very few teens listed faith or moral conviction as their reason for abstaining.)

In addition to the physical intimacy encouraged by different media sources, there is also another form of intimacy that is highly overlooked: emotional intimacy. Proverbs 4:23, "Above all else, guard your heart, for it is the wellspring of life." Students can guard their physical hearts but leave their emotional hearts wide open. Especially with the easy access of technology these days, students open up the deepest recesses of their hearts and display them on Facebook, Twitter, or even personal blogs. Emotional intimacy can be just as dangerous—if not more so—than physical intimacy. Teens need to be taught that no one should have access to their hearts through the use of a keypad.

---

5 Steps to Leading Your Teen Through Our Sexualized Culture

Step 1: Love them and be involved.
(Ask questions, keep them accountable, and encourage good choices and behavior.)

Step 2: Model spiritual growth and God's will and way for sex.
(As parents, openly discuss Bible studies and prayer life. Single parents demonstrate sexual purity in relationships by waiting.)

The more Steps 1–2 occur, the easier Steps 3–5 become.

Step 3: Teach and discuss God's plan for sex.
(Offer biblical counterexamples to media's depiction of sexual relationships and the behaviors observed elsewhere.)

Step 4: Identify and discuss the many good reasons for waiting.
(Point out examples whenever possible. The more children see the benefits, the more likely they are to see the validity of biblical teaching.)

Step 5: Help them establish relational boundaries.
(Even if they say they don't need it, children need guidance in creating boundaries and understanding their value.)

Biblical Perspectives on Sex
Genesis 1:27–28 (Original intent)
Genesis 2:18–27 (Intimacy)
2 Samuel 13:1–20 (Women as objects)
Proverbs 5 (Warnings of adultery)
Matthew 5:27–28 (Lustful desires)
1 Corinthians 6:9–7:9 (Sexual immorality/Sex within marriage)
1 Thessalonians 4:1–8 (Self-control)

Source of Conflict 4: Popularity and the "Coolness" Factor

> These days, popularity results less from sports success or even personal attractiveness, and more from being immersed in the "culture of cool," a media-saturated, consumer-driven state of pseudo adulthood. Childhood popularity now is dictated by materialism, competition and exposure to the adult world.[29]

Popularity is shifting from being achievement based to being experience based. Teens are learning earlier about things that were once off-limits or reserved for adults only. In addition, a new "coolness" factor is being introduced to our children involving consumption and materialism. Many retailers now admit that their number one target demographic is Generation Y (people between the ages of eight and twenty-six), and these young people are responding in big ways. In 2002, children between the ages of four and twelve spent more than $40 billion and influenced the household spending of more than $600 billion.[30]

Because of this alarming trend, students need to be educated about adult issues sooner rather than later. Topics such as money, advertising strategies, the true meaning of success, and a healthy perspective on what is important in life must all be taught at an early age. Please do not confuse ignorance with innocence. Educating children about mature issues will not encourage them to participate in those behaviors. When you teach your children to choose between right and wrong, you give them an invaluable tool that they can use for the rest of their lives.

Source of Conflict 5: The Influence of Friends

Several years ago, Group Publishing and Gallup research published a report on church satisfaction. The results echoed what many people had known for years: nearly three out of every four church members who worship with friends said their faith was involved in every aspect of their lives, whereas only about half the members who had no friends at church reported deep involvement in their faith. According to their research, the key component in raising lifelong disciples of Christ is *community*.[31] Teens and adults alike need to feel connected and part of a group. If students don't feel like they belong, then chances are, they will not believe.

Children's friends can exert a negative influence as well. The phrase "Show me your friends, and I'll show you your future" has a whole new meaning in this society. Children are very impressionable, so the friends with whom they choose to associate will have a tremendous effect on their spiritual growth.

In conclusion, children can overcome these sources of conflict and go on to write amazing stories with their lives, and parents are the primary agents who make that happen! As Dr. James Murphy of Davis College in Binghamton, New York, once said, "Change yourself, change your family, and you'll change the world." The families here at Journey of Faith Church can do just that!

Questions to Ponder and Discuss

1. How have you personally, and as a family, stepped out in faith this past year?

2. In what ways are you as a parent modeling a "sold-out" life for Jesus Christ?

3. Has your family adopted the "monk" or "miner" view of media consumption? What do you think are the advantages and disadvantages of both?

4. What types of technology do you allow into your home, and what are the rules governing that technology?

5. Do you know your children's friends and their parents? What are some ways that you are holding your children accountable in regard to their friendships?

Recommended Reading

Revolutionary Parenting by George Barna
Group's Emergency Response Handbook for Parents by Group Publishing
Bringing Up Boys and *Bringing Up Girls* by Dr. James Dobson

The Journey Continues ... Let's stop here for one more reminder: These stages or seasons are NOT always linear, and sometimes these passages of life overlap and become overpowering and all consuming. But you can be guaranteed of one thing you have picked up in several chapters—you matter to God. The depth of His love for you compelled Him to send His Son, Jesus, to the cross for your sins. The following chapter is all about responding to the precious gift of salvation and taking steps to grow in your faith. You are about to learn and possibly experience for the first time the season of rebirth. God be with you on the journey.

6

Rebirth:
I'm a Christian ... Now What?

Don Willett

*You can know and be assured of your salvation
by faith in what God has written.*

One of the best-loved books of all time is C. S. Lewis's *The Lion, the Witch, and the Wardrobe.* The basic elements of the Christian life are all presented there in imaginative ways, and adults and children alike find themselves drawn into the plot. The lion Aslan is the Christ-figure in the series, yet he isn't mentioned until well into the book. A talking Beaver first mentions Aslan to the young heroes of the series, four youngsters—Peter, Edmond, Susan, and Lucy—who are still new to the wintry world of Narnia. As the author describes it, each child reacts differently to Beaver's mention of Aslan:

> Beaver whispers, "They say Aslan is on the move—perhaps has already landed."
>
> And now a very curious thing happened. None of the children knew who Aslan was any more than you do; but the moment the Beaver had spoken these words everyone felt quite different ... At the name of Aslan each one of the children felt something jump in his inside. Edmond felt a sensation of mysterious horror. Peter felt suddenly brave and adventurous. Susan felt as if some delicious smell or some delightful strain of music had just floated by her. And Lucy got the feeling you have when you wake up in the morning and realize that is the beginning of the holidays or the beginning of summer.[32]

Leaving the fantasy world of Narnia and exploring your journey of faith in the here-and-now, know that you too will have your own unique story about how you first met Christ and how you came to follow Him more fully. In this chapter, I want to point your attention to a biblical "map" of the journey and highlight five key milestones that will be markers along your way forward.

And, yes, "Aslan is on the move." Today. And He wants to walk alongside you.

1. The Journey Begins—The Disciple's Assurance on the Journey

Though the four children—Peter, Edmond, Susan, and Lucy—each had a unique relationship with Aslan, *we* must realize that the journey begins for each believer the same way—with surrender to Christ. The *how* may differ, but it must be an authentic connection to Jesus. The believer's faith story begins when he or she discovers that "I have lost my way. I am exhausted ruling as king over my own domain. I need to know the One who designed me. There must be more to my life as I have known it. Lord, Jesus, You are that One that I have avoided and disregarded. I am so sorry. But I now know differently. You are all that I need. Please reign in my broken life. You are what matters. I receive your gift of salvation and relationship."

Saving Grace. Here is the first key milestone to mark the journey forward. In the Bible, grace can be understood as both saving grace and restorative grace. First, saving grace focuses on the fact that a believer's salvation is assured. Each of the following verses, all penned by the apostle John, emphatically teaches that the believer can be certain of God's love and forgiveness. Look at these verses closely for yourself. Own them. Personalize them. Amazing grace!

> John 3:36, 5:24: "*has* eternal life" [not hope to have, or might have].
> John 6:37, 39: "I will *certainly not* cast out … I lose nothing."
> John 10:27–29: "they will never perish, and *no one* will snatch them out of My hand … and *no one* is able to snatch them out of the Father's hand."
> 1 John 5:12–13: "These things I have written to you … so that you may *know* that you have eternal life."

You have eternal life (not *will* have or *hope* you have). God cannot *not* love you. You can know and be assured of your salvation by faith in what He has written. That salvation is irreversible and cannot be lost. As you move forward on the journey, you will need to learn to be confident in the truth of God's certain, unconditional, and undeserved love. Maybe you have looked in all the wrong places, and you know firsthand that you can't find God's kind of love anywhere or from anyone other than Him. So, we meet saving grace at the beginning of the journey. And you will return to the truth of this milestone again and again over the years. The powerful words of Christian psychologist Lewis Smeades may convince you that you are loved and accepted:

Grace overcomes shame, not by uncovering an overlooked cache of excellence in ourselves but simply accepting us, the whole of us, with no regard to our beauty or ugliness, our virtue or our vices. We are accepted wholesale. Accepted with no possibility of being rejected. Accepted once and accepted forever. Accepted at the ultimate depth of our being. We are given what we have longed for in every nook and nuance of every relationship.

We are ready for grace when we are bone tired of our struggle to be worthy and accepted. After we have tried too long to earn the approval of everyone important to us, we are ready for grace. When we are tired of trying to be the person somebody sometime convinced us we had to be, we are ready for grace. When we have given up all hope of our being an acceptable human being, we may hear in our hearts the ultimate reassurance: we are accepted, accepted by grace.[33]

Theologian J. I. Packer described how thoroughly and irreversibly God knows and loves the believer. Yet He is not disillusioned or surprised by what believers say, do, or think. "There is tremendous relief in knowing that His love of me is utterly realistic based at every point on prior knowledge of the worst about me, so that no discovery can now disillusion Him about me."[34]

A New Identity. As you travel on the journey of life, God invites you to see yourself as He does—not as other people see you. How does God see you? You are worthy of His love, and you are significant in His sight. You are eligible for His love, and His love is relentless, reliable, and restorative. You can enjoy your privileged status and immeasurable worth as a son or daughter of God.

Some seem to view salvation as a process that is somewhat like a judge dismissing the case against them and setting them free. There is so much more! Salvation sets you free from the confining cell that imprisoned you—so you can stand in the warm sunlight and breathe the fresh air on the outside for the first time. Once free, you must learn to establish a new life outside the prison walls and depend on the fact that God loves you, though He knows the worst about you. You are His son or daughter.

Caution—Profound Memory Loss. It is easy to forget who we are in Christ and not see ourselves as God sees us. After all, your enemy on the journey, the evil one, takes aim at your experience of God's grace and your new identity as His son or daughter. Now that you are saved, the Devil wants you to diminish the impact of God in your life.

Christian professors Gary Moon and David Benner in *Spiritual Direction and the Care of Souls* caution us that "Ever since the fall, we have shown a striking tendency to forget who we really are ... We have suffered a profound memory loss regarding how life is to be lived in friendship with God."[35]

Our spiritual growth will come to a halt when we forget who we are to Him. No wonder we believers are commanded to "Grow in the grace and knowledge of our Lord and Savior Jesus Christ" (2 Peter 3:18).

2. Baptism: "Under New Management"

A second vital milestone on the journey is your baptism. One of the distinctive marks of a disciple is his or her following Christ in baptism. Jesus's parting words in the "Great Commission" are found in Matthew 28:19–20.

> "Therefore go and make disciples of all nations, baptizing them in the name of the Father and of the Son and of the Holy Spirit, and teaching them to obey everything I have commanded you. And surely I am with you always, to the very end of the age."

In baptism, you announce that you are now the exclusive property of the Father, Son, and Holy Spirit. "In the name of" is a business term, signifying "ownership." You have seen a banner on a store announcing that it is now "Under New Management." The store has been sold, and the keys have been given to someone else who will now manage it. Baptism tells the public to expect to meet a new owner.

Jesus told His disciples to baptize new believers and teach them " 'to obey everything I have commanded you' " (Matthew 28:20a). Through baptism, you announce your departure from your old path, and the launch of a new journey. A new "map" will govern your journey—the reliable map of God's Word. A distinctively Christian lifestyle will emerge as you declare your willingness to be taught and to put into practice all that He has commanded in God's Word.

The public nature of baptism also stands out as a ceremony in which you identify yourself with other Christians. Baptism is no secret, private commitment to Christ. Rather, baptism momentarily throws the spotlight on the believer in front of friends, family, and the body of Christ. It is as if the person being baptized says, "I will need you on my journey." To which the onlookers reply, "We will walk together with you. You are one of us." Baptism is a very important milestone to understand and celebrate.

3. The Disciple's Transformation—Restorative Grace for the Journey

The third milestone to mark your path as a believer is restorative or regenerative grace. It is the process of becoming less bound to sin and more like Jesus Himself. Whereas salvation is the instantaneous and complete birth of your spiritual life, sanctification is the spiritual growth that comes over a lifetime. It is progressive and incomplete. No believer becomes holy in a hurry.

I often hear: "I'm a Christian. Now what?"

I find that question very refreshing and encouraging, because naming Jesus as Savior and Lord is not like crossing a finish line. Making that declaration of faith is instead the first step in a lifelong spiritual journey. Then we are to be formed, conformed, and transformed.

My dear children, for whom I am again in the pains of childbirth until Christ is *formed* in you (Galatians 4:19, emphasis mine).

For those God foreknew he also predestined to be *conformed* to the likeness of his Son, that he might be the firstborn among many brothers (Romans 8:29, emphasis mine).

And we, who with unveiled faces all reflect the Lord's glory, are being *transformed* into his likeness with ever-increasing glory, which comes from the Lord, who is the Spirit (2 Corinthians 3:18, emphasis mine).

Each of these verses shows the apostle Paul's fundamental conviction that we are to expect transformation, and that change is an ongoing process.

First and foremost, God loves His people unconditionally even though He is very aware of human sins, faults, shortcomings, and free will. Second, God's love is causeless (people can do nothing to earn or deserve it); ceaseless (He loved every person before birth, and He will never stop loving any of His children); and measureless (God's love is infinite, never changing, never ending). When you accept Jesus Christ as Savior and Lord, your sins are forgiven, and you can be eternally secure in God's love. We can be free of past hurts and grounded in the love God has for us. Our sense of significance and self-worth is based entirely and unshakably on our identity as God's son or daughter. Imagine the practical differences this new way of thinking can make in your life!

We who are followers of Christ are to be continually transformed by God's Spirit in deep and substantial ways so that we will be more like Jesus.

In *Invitation to a Journey,* Christian educator Robert Mulholland addresses the issue of spiritual growth, proposing that it is best understood as a journey of deepening personal growth from brokenness and bondage to wholeness and Christ-likeness.

When spirituality is viewed as a journey, however, the way to spiritual wholeness is seen to lie in an increasingly faithful response to the One whose purpose shapes our path, whose grace redeems our detours, whose power liberates us from our crippling bondages of the prior journey and whose transforming presence meets us at each turn in the road. In other words, spirituality is a pilgrimage of deepening responsiveness to God's control of our life and being.[36]

I have an answer to the "Now what?" question: We who are followers of Christ are to be continually transformed by God's Spirit in deep and substantial ways so that we will be more like Jesus. This dynamic growth process will take Christ's apprentices on a journey through three stages of spiritual development—childhood, young adulthood, and parenthood (1 John 2:12–14). Some are more mature and farther along than others.[37]

4. Getting in Shape for the Journey

Many of us have looked at ourselves in the mirror and said, "No way! It's time to get in shape! I need a membership at the gym." We sign up, get all fired up, get the Adidas bag, and then ... you know what happens. Attendance and enthusiasm begin to wane. And before long, the gym has our money but not our body. Here, the believer arrives at the fourth milestone.

Churches today desperately need believers who are in good spiritual shape, believers who are mature Christ followers. But according to Richard Foster, writer on Christian spirituality, that goal is quite countercultural. Commenting on the value our society places on immediate gratification—a value that opposes long-term, deep spiritual progress for the Christian— Foster has made the following insightful observation:

> Superficiality is the curse of our age. The doctrine of instant satisfaction is a primary spiritual problem. The desperate need today is not for more intelligent people nor gifted people, but for *deep* people.[38]

So what are we in the church to do for people to help them become *deep* and whole, transformed and not just informed? Journey of Faith is committed to discipling, educating, and preparing believers for the long haul of spiritual growth. But the leadership can't get in shape for you. And you can't hire a trainer to exercise for you. So sign up, get fired up, and bring your gym bag! It takes time to get—and stay—in shape. Paul Pettit, director of Spiritual Formation at Dallas Theological Seminary, suggests that authentic growth is indeed an ongoing and *lifelong* process. And he reminds us what spiritual growth is *not:*

> Make no mistake: maturing as a Christian is a process. It is not a second step, a higher plane, a sacred blessing, or a lightning bolt moment when God invades and brings the Christian to a perfected place. A lifelong transformation is set into motion when one places his or her faith in Jesus Christ and seeks to follow Him.[39]

So back to the question: What are we to do? How will you get in spiritual shape for the long haul? Journey of Faith offers small groups that are for sharing, study, and support. Take the initiative to find and develop friendships where you can be real and discard pretense and where others can walk with you. Know that isolation, the "Lone Ranger" model, never works. Spiritual growth is about "Jesus and me," as well as "Jesus and we." It is both personal and interpersonal. Share the story of your journey and invite others to live out the Christian experience with you. Many people at Journey of Faith will tell you that they are being transformed and becoming "deep" and whole because of these relationships.

Secondly, to get in spiritual shape, become friends with God. He has left believers with a "map"—the Word of God—to guide you on the journey. At the same time, getting in shape spiritually is not to be mistaken for just accumulating abstract doctrine or gaining a merely cognitive understanding of the Christian faith. Such efforts do not lead to wholeness or to Christ-likeness. Factual knowledge of God is incomplete without experiential knowledge of Him. You can't become "deep" and whole without the "word of God abiding in you" (1 John 2:14).

So take every opportunity that Journey of Faith offers to connect with biblical truths presented in the worship service, classes, and small groups. And read God's Word on your own. Your growth depends on it!

May I recommend a book that will help you develop exercises to get you in shape? Pastor and teacher Chuck Swindoll, in his book *So You Want to Be Like Christ? Eight Essentials to Get You There*, points to 1 Timothy 4:7, "*Discipline* yourself for the purpose of godliness." Paul selected the word *gymnazo*, from which we get our word *gymnasium*. The New American Standard Bible translates it as "discipline."

Each of the eight essentials Swindoll describes in his book is a different station in the gym where you can work out and get in great shape.[40] Each group of spiritual muscles will benefit from this workout in the soul's gymnasium:

1. Intimacy: Deepening Our Lives
2. Simplicity: Uncluttering Our Minds
3. Silence and Solitude: Slowing Our Pace
4. Surrender: Releasing Our Grip
5. Prayer: Calling Out
6. Humility: Bowing Low

7. Self-Control: Holding Back
8. Sacrifice: Giving Over

"It's time to get in shape! Let's go to God's gym!"

5. Sharing Your Faith on the Journey

The fifth milestone on the journey really is a continuation of the fourth one: Getting in Shape for the Journey. You have an opportunity to interact with many people, including your family, friends, neighbors, coworkers, the people you meet at your workplace, Starbucks—and ideally the gym. It was the apostle Peter who challenged the followers of Christ to understand their faith and to be ready to answer the searching questions of others: "Always be prepared to give an answer to everyone who asks you to give the reason for the hope that you have. But do this with gentleness and respect" (1 Peter 3:15).

People around us (including Christians) often make comments that can lead to discussions and deeper relationships. They may ask tough questions that challenge us to know what we believe and require us to know how to skillfully answer their questions without alienating them. Peter wanted us to guide others on the journey and to share our story—to make friends on God's behalf and to steer people to know Him. Of course, God is not expecting us to be the "Bible Answer Man or Woman."

In 1967, I became a Christian two weeks before my sophomore year in college began in upstate New York. I returned to campus, where I was to live in a fraternity house, and was surrounded by soccer and baseball players each day on the practice field. I was outnumbered and knew little about my faith. But I courageously shared my story and tried to live for Christ. When asked questions, I often didn't know the answers. But I learned to go to those who did. Do you know that my peers thought I was a Bible scholar because I could quote John 3:16? (That's how little people know.) I was a rookie. But I grew quickly as I kept in relationship with those around me.

Where did I get that determination? How did I learn so much about faith as a young Christian? In part, I was imitating the ardor and commitment of believers I looked up to. Also, I remember leaders talking about Douglas Hyde and his book *Dedication and Leadership,* in which he shares his experiences and the tactics of Communists in recruiting their members and training them into leaders.[41] *How did such a tiny minority accomplish so much?*

Douglas Hyde was a young man, living in London and aspiring to leadership in the Communist party. As a new recruit, he was told, "Here's some Party literature. Go on the public street corner and sell it." He was opposed to selling books in the street because it seemed beneath him. But he relented and took the literature to the streets, where he was mocked and encountered heated objections to Communism. He didn't realize how much he didn't know, but he remained in the fight. In discovering his own inadequacy, he felt compelled to learn the answers. Each time he returned to the streets, he was determined to do better. That's how leaders are made. (Doesn't that remind you of Jesus's selection of the first disciples and appointing them to be fishers of men?)

Hyde took classes taught by others who were working in the streets, and he reported that each class finished with these words: "What are you going to do with what you have learned today?" And the first item on the agenda when the class met next was always, "How did you apply what you learned last week?" Learning was connected with action.

Douglas Hyde later became a Christian, and he encouraged the church to use the same model for training as the Communists. His advice to us today? Take it to the streets. Share your faith, get involved, be committed, and in the process of giving your faith away, you will learn to answer questions because you are on the front lines.

As you continue your journey of life, please stop to examine and act on the milestones we've outlined: saving and restorative grace, baptism, spiritual fitness, and sharing your faith. Engage with other believers, seek wisdom in God's Word, and become conversant with His plan for your life. Share the story of salvation so that others too can know the joy you have found in Christ, and take up Peter's challenge:

> Always be prepared to give an answer to everyone who asks you to give the reason for the hope that you have. But do this with gentleness and respect (1 Peter 3:15).

Questions to Ponder and Discuss

1. In *The Lion, The Witch, and The Wardrobe*, Peter, Edmond, Susan, and Lucy each hear the same words about Aslan (the lion Christ-figure) for the first time from the Beaver. But they each have a different response to the message. As you think about your story of faith, what is one thing about Jesus that first attracted *you* to Him?

2. The first key milestone on the journey is the assurance of God's love and forgiveness. What in this section spoke to you about your own certainty of salvation? Explain your answer.

3. Do you ever forget how much God loves you? Does His love ever seem to diminish in your experience? What is one effect that forgetfulness has on you?

4. What is one area of your life where you would like to see change or experience God's healing touch? What is one difference that change might make? Be specific.

5. Richard Foster said, "Superficiality is the curse of our age. The doctrine of instant satisfaction is a primary spiritual problem. The desperate need today is not for more intelligent people nor gifted people, but for *deep* people." How could a small group or relationship with other believers help you become "deep" in your walk?

Recommended Reading

So You Want to Be Like Christ? Eight Essentials to Get You There by Chuck Swindoll
Stages of Faith: 8 Milestones That Mark Your Journey by Don Willett
TrueFaced: Trust God and Others with Who You Really Are by Bill Thrall, Bruce McNicol, and John Lynch

The Journey Continues ... When God awakens within the human heart a desire to know Him, another dimension of life is also awakened—the yearning to worship. The problem is that many people misunderstand the value of worship on the journey of life. May the following pages begin your awakening to a season of worship in life to comfort and lead you through the other seasons as well.

7

Worship:
An Indispensable Part of
Our Journey of Life

Mark Portis

*To live a life of worship means that we surrender
our will, our way of doing things,
to God's higher ways.*

Worship. A word loaded with meaning and easily misunderstood, especially during the times in which we live. Is it a church service? Is it the set of songs before the message? Is it an emotional experience we have when we're singing and feel close to God? Is it a genre or type of music? Is it a lifestyle?

We will address these and other questions in this chapter. We'll also look at some of the ways that worship practices can become misdirected—even idolatrous—if we're not careful.

What Is Worship?

One of the best definitions of *worship* I've found comes from William Temple, the late Archbishop of Canterbury. Here is a condensed version:

> To worship is to quicken the conscience by the holiness of God,
> to feed the mind with the truth of God,
> to purge the imagination by the beauty of God,
> to open the heart to the love of God,
> to devote the will to the purpose of God.[42]

No definition is complete, but there are some important things we can learn as we work our way through Temple's words and look at Scriptures that speak to these different expressions of worship.

"To Quicken the Conscience by the Holiness of God." *Quicken* is not a word we use a lot these days, unless we're talking about the popular computer software. One dictionary defines the word this way: "to stimulate, awaken, revive." So, as it relates to worship, it means that our consciences are awakened by God's holiness. In other words, the closer you get to God, the more aware you become of how holy He is and how sinful you are.

The prophet Isaiah encountered God in this way:

> In the year that King Uzziah died, I saw the Lord seated on a throne, high and exalted, and the train of his robe filled the temple. Above him were seraphs, each with six wings: With two wings they covered their faces, with two they covered their feet, and with two they were

flying. And they were calling to one another: "Holy, holy, holy is the Lord Almighty; the whole earth is full of his glory." At the sound of their voices the doorposts and thresholds shook and the temple was filled with smoke. "Woe to me!" I cried. "I am ruined! For I am a man of unclean lips, and I live among a people of unclean lips, and my eyes have seen the King, the Lord Almighty" (Isaiah 6:1–5).

Isaiah is then touched by the grace of God and, rising up, responds to God's request by declaring that he's willing to go anywhere God might choose to send him.

Although it's important that we recognize our sinfulness, it's never God's intention that we stay there, wallowing in guilt. Psalm 34:5 encourages us by saying, "Those who look to him are radiant; their faces are never covered with shame." The grace of God is a powerful thing, even more potent than a list of regrets or the haunting memory of a selfish choice that brought pain to you and others. His grace can cover it all.

So, the beginning point of worship is to understand who God is and who we are in relationship to Him. We are to approach Him humbly, in reverence and with a contrite heart.

"To Feed the Mind with the Truth of God." How can we rightly worship God if we don't know Him through His revealed Word? In addition to Sunday morning sermons, regular reading and study of God's Word will help us keep an accurate picture of who God is and what it means to worship Him. Here are a couple of Scriptures that speak of this:

Blessed is the man who does not walk in the counsel of the wicked or stand in the way of sinners or sit in the seat of mockers. But his delight is in the law of the LORD, and on his law he meditates day and night (Psalm 1:1–2).

The law of the LORD is perfect, reviving the soul. The statutes of the LORD are trustworthy, making wise the simple. The precepts of the LORD are right, giving joy to the heart. The commands of the LORD are radiant, giving light to the eyes. The fear of the LORD is pure, enduring forever. The ordinances of the LORD are sure and altogether righteous (Psalm 19:7–9).

Although there is certainly a place for emotions and feelings in worship, these passages remind us that our lives are to be in accordance with the written Word of God. He is to be worshipped in both spirit and truth.

"To Purge the Imagination by the Beauty of God." This quality of worship (according to Temple's definition) may especially resonate with those who enjoy the arts, love the beauty of God's creation, or just tend to be a little more "right brained" in general. We serve an unbelievably creative God whose handiwork is all around us. A spectacular sunset, an unexpected rainbow, the birth of a child—these are moments that often elicit worship.

The imagination is a powerful thing. It is often associated with thoughts or images that are less than godly. Theologian Warren Wiersbe cautions, "Unless imagination is held captive to the truth of God's Word, it will lead us astray."[43] That's why it's important for us to remember the exhortation in Philippians 4:8 that "Whatever is true, whatever is noble, whatever is right, whatever is pure, whatever is lovely, whatever is admirable—if anything is excellent or praiseworthy, think about such things."

Music and other art forms can allow our minds and imaginations to be captured by the beauty of God because they tap into our emotions and spirits differently than the spoken word. The author and lay theologian C. S. Lewis referred to the imagination as "the organ of meaning,"[44] and we would be wise to not ignore it or be fearful of it, but rather ask God to sanctify our imaginations for His glory.

"To Open the Heart to the Love of God." Simply receiving the love of God can be an act of worship. The apostle Paul writes passionately about this in his letter to the church of Ephesus:

> I pray that out of his glorious riches he may strengthen you with power through his Spirit in your inner being, so that Christ may dwell in your hearts through faith. And I pray that you, being rooted and established in love, may have power, together with all the saints, to grasp how wide and long and high and deep is the love of Christ, and to know this

love that surpasses knowledge—that you may be filled to the measure of all the fullness of God (Ephesians 3:16–19).

According to Paul, receiving the love of God causes us to be filled up "to the measure of all the fullness of God."

The truth is that it's difficult for many of us to fathom God's unconditional love for us. His love is so much higher and purer than anything we can experience here on earth that it seems almost incomprehensible. Also, we're so aware of our shortcomings, pride, and many *unlovable* qualities that it's hard to believe He really loves us just the way we are. But He does. Really. And the act of receiving that amazing love is an often overlooked but vitally important facet of worship.

"To Devote the Will to the Purpose of God." Remember Isaiah? Once he was touched by the supernatural grace and forgiveness of God, he was ready for anything. The Lord called out, "Whom shall I send? And who will go for us?" Isaiah responded, "Here I am, send me."

I can remember at the age of twenty-two, bowing down on the cold floor of a rustic cabin in the San Bernardino Mountains and praying a similar prayer. I could sense that God was calling me into the ministry, and I told Him that I wanted to serve Him with all my heart. I also asked Him to never let me forget that moment. I haven't.

To live a life of worship means that we surrender our will, our way of doing things, to God's higher ways. This may sound simple, but this process of sanctification is lifelong and requires humility, submission, and an acknowledgment that God's ways are better than our ways. It also means living in the larger story of God bringing about His kingdom here on earth as it is in heaven.

All of this comes down to daily choices, so let's look now at some of the aspects of worship in the life of a believer.

Worship in the Life of a Believer

Expressing Worship in Obedient Devotion. Consider the following passage: "Offer your bodies as living sacrifices ... this is your spiritual act of worship" (Romans 12:1). The Greek word used for worship in the above passage, *Latreuo*, literally means "to serve in an obedient and sacrificial way." Obeying God and making sure we're right with others is not usually what we think of as worship. But this is where the rubber meets the road.

It's amazing how neglectful—or even rebellious—we can be in our relationship with God during the week. But when Sunday rolls around, our arms are raised, our eyes are closed, and we're lost in the wonder of praise. You have to wonder what God thinks about that.

I've been married for almost twenty years to my beautiful wife, Linda. I love her very much, and I know that she loves me. Let's imagine that throughout the course of a week, I repeatedly ignored her requests, made no effort to communicate with her, and actually did things that I knew would cause her pain. Then on Friday night, at the end of the week, I suddenly dimmed the lights, put on a little music, and started to sing her love songs. Do you think she would accept my "offering"? It's highly doubtful, and why should she—until I listen to her heart, confess my behavior, and seek her forgiveness?

Does this mean our lives have to be perfect and blameless before we can truly worship God? No. But He does ask us to be honest before Him, confessing our sins regularly and then continuing to pursue an obedient lifestyle. We come to Him as we are—broken, hurting, dry, and discouraged. He meets us where we are. We worship a forgiving God who is always ready to meet our needs, restore us, and renew our hearts. We just need to go to Him—ready and willing.

Offering More Meaningful Worship by Growing Our Relationship with God. We've seen that worship is expressed in a life of obedient service and devotion. However, in addition to serving God, we need to know Him and be growing in our relationship with Him. Again, the apostle Paul has some very personal words to share here.

But whatever was to my profit I now consider loss for the sake of Christ. What is more, I consider everything a loss compared to the surpassing greatness of knowing Christ Jesus my Lord, for whose sake I have lost all things. I consider them rubbish, that I may gain Christ and be found in him, not having a righteousness of my own that comes from the law, but that which is through faith in Christ—the righteousness that comes from God and is by faith. I want to know Christ and the power of his resurrection and the fellowship of sharing in his sufferings, becoming like him in his death, and so, somehow, to attain to the resurrection from the dead (Philippians 3:7–11).

In 2002, while I was on staff at Lake Avenue Church, I was granted some sabbatical time. I was grateful for the opportunity to set aside all of the "doing" for a period of time and just "be." It was time to be alone, time to be with Linda and the boys, and time to get to know God and His Word better. During those few months, Philippians 3 really came alive for me. I felt I was getting to know God in a way that I never had before. The times of solitude were refreshing to my soul and helped carve out a space in my spirit where I could meet with God and hear from Him, at times with almost shocking clarity.

Music and other art forms can allow our minds and imaginations to be captured by the beauty of God because they tap into our emotions and spirits differently than the spoken word.

One of the phrases from Scripture that caught my attention early on was to "fix my eyes on Jesus" from the well-known passage in Hebrews (12:2). A few weeks later, I had Lasik surgery to correct vision in both my eyes. There were some complications, and I nearly lost my eyesight for about ten days. I couldn't drive, watch television, or even read. It was a very helpless feeling.

But through that trial, God met me in a uniquely profound way. Not only did He eventually "fix my eyes" as my vision returned, but He opened them to new insights about my relationship with Him and with others. He also downloaded the inspiration to write several songs and gave me a new, fresh outlook on ministry. I realized that even though I had been called to be a "worship leader" that I was first and foremost a "worshipper" and a son of the King. It was freeing, humbling, and energizing at the same time.

More than anything, worship is a response to God—to who He is and what He's done for us. It should never be seen as mere duty or obligation. We respond to God and love Him. Why? Because He first loved us.

Because He saved us, restored us, rescued us, redeemed us, delivered us, healed us, and is preparing a place for us to live with Him forever!

Generating and Sustaining Worship Through the Holy Spirit. Lastly, as we think about worship in the life of a believer, we need to remember that it's not something done with our own strength, as a work of our own flesh. Rather, it must be enabled and fueled by the Holy Spirit. Well-known Christian author A. W. Tozer writes, "It is impossible for any of us to worship God without the impartation of the Holy Spirit. It is the operation of the Spirit of God within us that enables us to worship God acceptably through that Person we call Jesus Christ, who is Himself God."[45]

The Holy Spirit prompts us, guides us, and provides the passion and fuel for us to worship God. Paul talks a lot about this in Galatians 5—living by the Spirit, keeping in step with the Spirit, and being led by the Spirit. If our lives are Spirit controlled, then the evidence will be lives filled with the fruit of the Spirit: love, joy, peace, patience, kindness, goodness, faithfulness, gentleness, and self-control.

Why is this so important? Because left to ourselves, our service—even if it's done in the "name of the Lord"—can be done for all kinds of wrong reasons, including these:

1. Out of duty or obligation or pressure from others
2. So that others will think more highly of us
3. To "earn points" with God
4. To feel good about ourselves

So, now that we understand some of the aspects of worship in the life of an individual believer, let's take a look at how worship is expressed in the context of a community of believers.

Worship in the Life of a Community

Although the Bible does not give us a *blueprint* of what every worship service should look like, it does provide several examples of corporate worship gatherings.

Worship in Community Should Be Inclusive and Orderly. Worship in community is primarily for believers, but there should always be an awareness that *seekers* are likely to be there and should feel welcome. Some churches have taken this to the extreme and chosen to make their services "seeker oriented" or even "seeker driven." These services are designed specifically to attract unbelievers. Fortunately, these types of services have become less common. Worship gatherings should be designed primarily for believers to offer adoration and praise to God, but they should also be accessible to the unbeliever.

We don't want to be so quirky or elitist that others don't know what's going on or end up feeling as though they have just entered some exclusive club. On the other hand, Paul shows us a compelling picture of the church "being the church" in 1 Corinthians 14 where the result is unbelievers being astonished and "convicted of sin and brought under judgment by all, as the secrets of their hearts are laid bare. So they will fall down and worship God, exclaiming, 'God is really among you!' " (1 Corinthians 14:24–25).

In that same chapter, the concept of orderliness in worship is also addressed. Verse 33 says, "God is not a God of disorder but of peace." And verse 40 says "… everything should be done in a fitting and orderly way." Worship gatherings should not be marked by chaos or seen as a free-for-all. They should be thoughtfully and prayerfully planned and led. A sense of order and purpose can create an atmosphere in which people are able to focus on God instead of wondering what's coming next.

Worship in Community Requires Honesty and Humility. We certainly see this taught as it relates to the taking of Communion (1 Corinthians 11:27–28). I believe it also applies to our gatherings in general. Verses such as "I want men everywhere to lift up holy hands in prayer, without anger or disputing" (1 Timothy 2:8) remind us that God cares about what's going on in our hearts, and that we can't separate our attitudes toward others from our public demonstrations of worship. If we do, we're being dishonest, and we're compromising the very message of the gospel. Scripture is clear that God's heart is grieved by things such as disunity and pride. He values humility and authenticity and exhorts us in His Word to "Be completely humble and gentle; be patient, bearing with one another in love" (Ephesians 4:2).

Worship in Community Should Unify. Ephesians 4 continues: "Make every effort to keep the unity of the Spirit through the bond of peace. There is one body and one Spirit—just as you were called to one hope when you were called" (Ephesians 4:3). When God says, "make every effort," it seems we should pay attention. Jesus prayed for us as believers that we would be one, " 'just as you are in me and I am in you' " (John 17:21b). In the verses that follow, it becomes clear that this spirit of unity isn't just for our sake but also so that others may come to Christ as a result of how we love and care for each other.

Worship in Community Should Advance the Kingdom of God. Spiritual warfare is an aspect of worship that we don't tend to talk about very often, but it is real. You can bet that our enemy, Satan, hates it when the people of God gather to worship the one, true God. He would love nothing more than for us to argue about song selection or how well we liked the sermon and, in the process, forget the real reason why we've gathered together. He knows that when we get distracted and start to lose focus, we are spiritually dropping our swords and neglecting to bring honor and glory to our commander and chief, God Almighty.

One of the most vivid examples of worship "pushing back the darkness" is found in 2 Chronicles where King Jehoshaphat leads his army, as a worshipping choir, into battle, and God gives them the victory.

> As they set out, Jehoshaphat stood and said, "Listen to me, Judah and people of Jerusalem! Have faith in the LORD your God and you will be upheld; have faith in his prophets and you will be successful." After consulting the people, Jehoshaphat appointed men to sing to the LORD and to praise him for the splendor of his holiness as they went out at the head of the army, saying: "Give thanks to the LORD, for his love endures forever." As they began to sing and praise, the LORD set ambushes against the men of Ammon and Moab and Mount Seir who were invading Judah, and they were defeated (2 Chronicles 20:20b–22).

Most of us don't think of ourselves as warriors, and we prefer the idea of peace over war. But the reality is, if you're a worshipper of the living

God, then you're already engaged in war with the enemy of your soul. When we gather for worship, let's remember that we have the opportunity to stand firm on the Word of God, declaring that He's the only way and that His kingdom alone will last forever.

Worship in Community Should Declare the Greatness of God. Have you ever had the sense during a worship service, while singing a song about the holiness and glory of God, that *this* is what worship is all about? In the final analysis, it's not about you or us or even our church. It's about God Himself. The One on the throne. The One whom we will worship forever!

The Psalms are filled with verses proclaiming the wonder and majesty of God. Here's one example:

> I will sing of the LORD's great love forever; with my mouth I will make your faithfulness known through all generations. ... The heavens praise your wonders, LORD, your faithfulness too, in the assembly of the holy ones. For who in the skies above can compare with the LORD? Who is like the LORD among the heavenly beings? In the council of the holy ones God is greatly feared; he is more awesome than all who surround him. Who is like you, LORD God Almighty? You, LORD, are mighty, and your faithfulness surrounds you (Psalm 89:1, 5–8).

How critical it is, when we gather as God's people for worship, that we make sure to celebrate our Triune God, declaring His attributes and extolling His virtues. Not just for what He has done, but for who He is.

Beware: The Idols of Worship

While we would be hard-pressed these days to find any Protestant, evangelical churches worshipping golden calves or bowing down before statues, we should be mindful of hidden idols and avoid them. The dictionary on my iMac defines *idol* this way: "An image or representation of a god used as an object of worship." In his book *Counterfeit Gods*, Pastor Tim Keller identifies an idol as "anything more important to you than

God, anything that absorbs your heart and imagination more than God, anything you seek to give you what only God can give."[46] So, let's consider for the next few moments the sobering reality that even the practice of worshipping God in community can become idolatrous, if we're not careful.

The Idol of Form. The forms of worship practices seem endless: contemporary, traditional, liturgical, charismatic, Pentecostal, blended, alternative, emergent, guitar led, piano driven, contemplative, celebratory ... the list goes on and on. Each form has its own "defenders" or "protectors." Churches have split over this kind of thing, so it can be a big deal.

Personally, I see value in different forms of worship. The Old and New Testaments present many different examples of God's people assembling for a particular event, dedication, or service, so it's hard to make a case that worship should *always* look a particular way. There's wisdom in drawing from a wide range of traditions. God Himself is so amazing and creative, why would we choose just one particular way to worship Him?

Although the Bible doesn't reveal exactly how we are to worship God on a weekly basis, it's clear that the form of worship is secondary to what's going on in the hearts and lives of the worshippers. Here are some examples from Scripture:

"I hate, I despise your religious feasts; I cannot stand your assemblies. Even though you bring me burnt offerings and grain offerings, I will not accept them. Though you bring choice fellowship offerings, I will have no regard for them. Away with the noise of your songs! I will not listen to the music of your harps. But let justice roll on like a river, righteousness like a never-failing stream!" (Amos 5:21–24).

The Lord says: "These people come near to me with their mouth and honor me with their lips, but their hearts are far from me. Their worship of me is made up only of rules taught by men" (Isaiah 29:13).

If we allow our method of worshipping God to become more important than our relationship with Him—or even more of a priority than our relationship with others—we have, on some level, made *form* an idol.

The Idol of Individualism. In a culture that celebrates individual achievement, it's easy to forget that worship in community is just that: a communal, shared event. It is not just a bunch of individuals gathering to have their own private time with God. You have the rest of the week for that. This is a time for the body of Christ to enter into the shared, cooperative experience of collectively giving thanks and praise to our God.

When we start thinking that worship is all about *us*—when we allow our preferences to take priority—we lose sight of what's important. And that's when the nitpicking begins: "I don't like that song." "Why is *she* up there singing?" "Why don't we just sing hymns and forget these new songs?" "I wish they had let me pick the color of the carpet." "This service better end soon or I'm going to miss my lunch reservation." It can get ridiculous, right?

People naturally bring different perspectives and preferences to church. But it's important to remember that worship is for God, not us. Imagine that you're going to Disneyland for the day, and there are only two of you. Although you may occasionally disagree on what ride to go on or where to eat, it should be relatively easy to reach a consensus (unless one of you is particularly stubborn!). Now imagine that a group of twelve is going to Disneyland. Unless you decide to split up, you may likely have a much harder time making decisions that please everybody. You now have twelve opinions to consider rather than only two. So it would be easy for the group to fracture or cave in to the self-appointed "leader."

You can probably see where I'm going with this. Apply the dynamics of those two scenarios to a worship service. Can you imagine trying to accommodate not twelve people but hundreds?

Ephesians 5:19–21 addresses this issue: "Speak to one another with psalms, hymns and spiritual songs. Sing and make music in your heart to the Lord, always giving thanks to God the Father for everything, in the name of our Lord Jesus Christ. Submit to one another out of reverence for Christ." Submitting to one another out of reverence for Christ. Has a nice ring to it, huh? Easier said than done though—unless we're being led by the Spirit, setting aside our personal preferences, and clothing ourselves with a spirit of mutual submission.

The Idol of Experience. This is where we allow our *feelings* to run the show.

1. "I don't 'feel' like worshipping." Throughout the book of Psalms we find both invitations and commands to "come and bless the Lord." When? Just when we feel like it? No, the Bible says we should do so "at all times." Author Eugene Peterson puts it this way:

> Many think that the only way to change your behavior is to change your feelings. But there is an older wisdom that puts it differently: By changing our behavior, we can change our feelings. One person says— "I don't feel like worshiping, therefore I'm not going to go to church." While another person says—"I don't feel like worshiping, therefore I will go to church and put myself in the way of worship." In the process, they find themselves blessed, and begin, in turn, to bless.[47]

If we choose to worship only when we feel like it, we have allowed our feelings to determine our actions rather than the other way around.

2. "I hope my worship 'experience' is as good as last week." It is very common for people to talk about an encounter they had with God during a church service or event. Although this isn't necessarily bad, it becomes an idol if it's the only gauge you use to determine whether you have worshipped God.

Worship leaders can be guilty of playing into this. We can set up a flow of songs to create "holy moments," and then evaluate the effectiveness of the worship time based on questions such as "How did the people respond? How many hands were raised?" Or the question I've heard asked: "Did we get there?" Where? Where are we trying to get again? And even if there is a *where*, is it realistic to think that all of us are going get there at the same time? If the experience itself becomes the goal, then God ceases to be at the center of our worship. This doesn't mean that feelings and experiences aren't a part of worship: it just means that they're a by-product—not the goal.

At this point, I'd like you to hear from Nate Carpenter, associate pastor of worship here at Journey, regarding many of the aspects of worship that we've been talking about, and how they're being "worked out" in the lives of many of our students.

A New Generation of Worshippers (Nate Carpenter)

But you are a chosen people, a royal priesthood, a holy nation, God's special possession, that you may declare the praises of him who called you out of darkness and into his wonderful light (1 Peter 2:9).

The verse above is one that has been on my heart this past year as I have led worship for the next generation in our church. So many young people in the past (myself included) have been an afterthought. They are being told that they are the church of tomorrow, and they will be amazing worshippers, prayer warriors, leaders, etc.—in the future. In actuality, we may learn some things from the next generation, as many of them are shining examples of what a worshipper is. Their lives of worship are reflected in the truth of 1 Peter 2:9 as they recognize that they have been chosen.

With a passionate thirst for what God has for them, these young people desire to worship Him with every opportunity they have. Worship services are one avenue, and they make the most of it. Once a month, more than 200 students from churches around the South Bay join together to worship God and pray for the community at a nightly gathering we call "Wowship." One eighth grader says it this way: "Come ready to put yourself aside and praise God." What an encouraging thing to see young people passionate about worshipping their Creator, instead of themselves. In addition, four times a year, the junior high ministry ("Ignite") has an all-worship service where they can pour out their worship to God in a variety of creative ways, including singing, writing, sculpting, or making bracelets. Many students say this is their favorite group activity. As young teenagers, you might assume their favorite part of church is the games, seeing their secret crush, or getting the candy. However, our surveys show that many of the students are most passionate about worshipping God.

95

That said, this new generation of worshippers seeks to express their worship in more ways than just singing. Through service projects on Saturdays, prayer groups, or witnessing on school campuses, the youth of today grasp something far deeper about worship than many of us did at their age. They understand that "it's not about me."

As we've been learning throughout this chapter, worship is not just singing our praise to God: it's a way of life. Our young people are saying, "Whether I am on the soccer field, in the classroom, or at work, may I give worship and praise to Christ. May we be a generation that longs to be passionate worshippers."

" 'Yet a time is coming and has now come when the true worshipers will worship the Father in spirit and in truth, for they are the kind of worshipers the Father seeks' " (John 4:23). This is the cry of the next generation. This is a call to a life of worship.

Welcome to the Banquet

As I draw this chapter to a close, I'd like to leave you with a picture. Imagine that all of us have gathered for a feast, each bringing our best offering. One person has brought a beautiful salad. Another has brought fresh-baked bread, and another has brought vine-ripened tomatoes, grown in his own garden. It's clear that no such feast would be possible without the offerings of all who have come to enjoy the occasion.

After everyone places their offering on the table, they are seated. But one seat is left open. Christ enters and sits at the head of the table. There is a moment of silence, followed by the Lord's Prayer spoken by Jesus Himself as He holds up a piece of warm bread. Everyone is enjoying the food and each other's company. Although people tend to prefer some dishes over others, that is secondary to the fellowship experienced around the table.

At a certain point in the meal, it becomes clear that one thing is of the utmost importance. The primary question on everyone's minds is whether Christ will be pleased with the meal. All of the individuals have their own favorite dishes. But that's not what matters. The much more important questions are "What does Jesus think about my offering? Will He be pleased? Did I offer my best? Have I withheld anything from my Savior?"

Can you imagine what our services would be like if we all came in with that perspective? Through our worship, may God be glorified as we seek to honor Him with all of our hearts, souls, minds, and strength. Amen!

Questions to Ponder and Discuss

1. Which aspect of the definition of *worship* provided by William Temple, the late Archbishop of Canterbury, resonated with you most? Which one is the most difficult for you to grasp or live out on a daily basis?

2. Worship, as it's expressed in the life of a believer, is characterized by obedience, growth, and living a spirit-filled life. What obstacles have you encountered in the past as you've sought to live in this way? List two or three ways you can cultivate a lifestyle of worship.

3. What is one new insight you gained from the section "Worship in the Life of a Community"? In what specific ways has this section challenged you to better understand your role as a participant in corporate worship gatherings?

4. Is there an "idol" of worship that you've been susceptible to in the past? What steps can you take to not fall into the same trap of idolatry?

5. What encourages you most about the next generation's passion for worship? In what ways do you feel challenged or convicted?

Recommended Reading

Whatever Happened to Worship? by A. W. Tozer
Real Worship by Warren Wiersbe
The Unquenchable Worshiper by Matt Redman

The Journey Continues ... You now understand how worship creates a greater sense of intimacy with your Lord. But did you know that accompanying this deeper yearning in your heart to know God is a greater desire to communicate with Him? God has provided a means for fulfilling this desire through what you will learn in the next chapter. Turn the page and prepare to develop the spiritual discipline of prayer—to have profound confidence in God's presence and leading as He walks with you on your journey.

8

Prayer:
Learning to Talk with Your Heavenly Father

Glen Martin

True prayer starts in the heart of God.
He then, through the Holy Spirit,
communicates this to our hearts.

When our children were first learning to drive, my wife, Nancy, would continually remind them to never allow the fuel gauge to register below one-quarter of a tank. She "nagged" them for a reason: I regularly drive on or near empty, and it drives her crazy. I rarely stop at a gas station until Nancy refuses to go any farther on our car's empty tank. It's not that driving on fumes is entertaining or exciting; it's just not something I think about all the time—and this has cost me.

Many people don't just drive on fumes: they live the Christian life on fumes. Their tanks are near empty due to a lack of refueling by the Scriptures. They cannot sleep because their lives are prayer-less and they lack an understanding of God's faithfulness. You may feel like so many others—that your only wish is to coast into church each Sunday with the hope that you can "fill up" with the Holy Spirit and make it through the journey of life for another week.

Why Don't We Pray?

I have discovered three reasons for this feeling of emptiness in the lives of so many Christians. First, they never set aside the time necessary to fill their tanks. "Glen, I just don't have a spare hour to spend with God right now." I didn't say an hour or even a half hour. But couldn't you find some time every day to allow prayer to make a difference? Instead, people declare, "Because I don't have a lot of time, I'm not going to give any time."

Second, people fail to find a place to reflect and be still. Could you find a place away from all the other stuff going on? Can you get away from the phone, the doorbell, and the kids even for a short time? If a relationship is important to us, we will get away from the crowd and focus on it. Do you know our problem, though? We like to multitask because we think that is most efficient. So we pray while we're driving or listening to a CD or shaving, all the while thinking, "Wow, four things at once, good use of my time." But what are our prayers really going to be like? When Jesus said go into your room and close your door, I don't think He was talking about being in your car.

Third, the simplicity of prayer has been lost. Because of our cultural, traditional, or historic approaches to God, we struggle with the concept of talking to Him as our friend. We start believing there are "right words" for our prayers, a correct posture to maintain, and many other aspects of prayer that will increase our confidence that God is listening.

Relationships Demand Communication

Most of us would agree that a relationship can only be as strong as the communication that takes place within it. Therefore, prayer is essential to our walk with God because it is the means by which we communicate back to Him. At Journey of Faith, we often affirm the truth God has communicated to us in a very specific and powerful way—through His Word, the Bible. Every single week, we gather together to learn the truth God desires to share with us. But we also realize that any communication that goes only one way is a monologue—not a dialogue. Thankfully, God has given us a means by which we can communicate back to Him, and it is called prayer. I'm convinced that it is through prayer that our relationship with God becomes real. If you are like me, though, many questions for God will come to mind—questions such as "When are You going to tell us how to make prayer really work?"

Have you ever put your money in a machine anticipating a cold drink, a candy bar, or a newspaper? Money in, item out—it seems so simple. But when it doesn't deliver the product purchased, you are tempted to give it a shake or thump, and frustration grows. If someone asked you at that moment what you think of vending machines, you'd probably answer, "I hate them. They don't work." I wonder how many Christians feel that way about God and see Him as their heavenly ATM. We put in our "prayer card" and expect God to roll out the twenty-dollar bills. If He doesn't work that way, or the screen says, "One moment, please," we wonder why we should even try.

Someone once said, "Prayer is not the process by which we bring God into our way of thinking, but rather the way in which He brings us into *His* way of thinking." The first rule of communication is to know your audience. This is not a problem with God. He has told us about Himself in the Bible, and He knows us even better than we know ourselves. So if there is ever a breakdown in the communication process, it is never because God misunderstands us. God knows everything about us—past, present, and future. More often, a problem happens in our prayers when we forget whom we are talking to.

Let's travel back to a time in the lives of the apostles when they walked with our Lord. They were so in awe of what they had seen in the prayer life of the Lord Jesus Christ that they went to Him and asked for some help: "Lord, teach us to pray," they said. "Lord, would you help us to capture the means by which You seem to connect with God, the Father?" Jesus gave them what we now call the Lord's Prayer. Within the framework of three great movements of prayer, our Lord outlined for these struggling disciples how to be sure God would listen, and how to have a prayer life with both impact and fulfillment. Jesus told the disciples, "You do not have to live your life on empty. I will teach you a model to follow to guarantee you will never again live the Christian life on fumes."

Lord, Teach Me to Pray

The opening words of the Lord's Prayer are compelling:

> "This is how you should pray: 'Our Father in heaven, hallowed be your name, your kingdom come, your will be done on earth as it is in heaven. Give us today our daily bread. Forgive us our debts, as we also have forgiven our debtors. And lead us not into temptation, but deliver us from the evil one' " (Matthew 6:9–13).

I know there's a temptation in prayer to wonder when we are going to get to the good part—the part where we tell God what we need. We're not ready to do that until we understand the beginning of this prayer. I know there's another temptation to think that if our Lord gave us this model, we should just memorize it and recite it whenever we get together. If this is the code by which we crack God's ATM, let's just learn the words and repeat them over and over again. Well, our Lord called that babbling. " 'And when you pray, do not keep on babbling like pagans, for they think they will be heard because of their many words' " (Matthew 6:7). The same words used time and again can lose potency over time.

Let me illustrate. Nancy and I have been married since 1974, and she loves to hear me say, "Honey, I love you." I've tried to use the "I've told you I love you, and if I ever change my mind, I'll let you know." But that just doesn't cut it. Nancy has always been very affectionate and can easily say to me, "Glen, I love you." But my response for a long time was "I love you—too." I might just as well have said "Ditto!" I think that when a woman says, "I love you," it triggers an immediate reaction in a man's brain: *incoming emotional statement.* The response becomes automatic. So when Nancy would say, "I love you," I was ready with a programmed reply: "I love you too."

We do that with prayer. Once we have the words down, we don't feel that we even need to stop what we're doing to pray. We forget that our Lord did not give us a script. He gave us a model.

> *So why would He invite us to pray? Because He loves us so much. We matter so much to God that He will listen to us at any hour - day or night.*

Getting God's Attention in Prayer

To get God's attention in prayer, our Lord lets us in on four steps.

Step 1. First, God views His children through the eyes of a loving Father. After Jesus's initial instruction, His opening words are tender and instructive: "This is how you should pray: 'Our Father in heaven' " (Matthew 6:9a). To hear this comment in the first century would have floored you. Just search the Old Testament and you'll soon see that the people of Israel never thought of God as their father. In fact, in John 8, in one of the verbal exchanges between Jesus and the Jewish leaders, they came to Him and challenged His authority to make the bold statements He was making. The Jewish leadership asked Jesus, "Who is your father?" Our Lord turned the question back on them and asked, "Well, who is yours?" They answered, "Abraham is our father." And Jesus shattered their conception of who He was in John 8:58–59: " 'I tell you the truth,' Jesus answered, 'before Abraham was born, I am!' At this, they picked up stones to stone him, but Jesus hid himself, slipping away from the temple grounds."

Can't you sense the tension? They could not accept that Jesus Christ was the eternal, preexistent God and that He had come to reveal the God of this universe to humankind in a very real and personal way. He's not our grandfather, not a kindly but out-of-touch power in the universe who issues decrees. He's our Father, who hears what His children want and understands that what they want is not always what they need. A father's love will drive Him to say "Yes" as often as He can, but He must do the right thing for them. Our Lord says that when we pray, we must understand that He is a personal God. And I must ask you today, "Is He your father in heaven?" John 1:12 reminds us, "Yet to all who received him, to those who believed in his name, he gave the right to become children of God."

You can be adopted into God's family with a simple surrender of your independence and an admission that you're lost without His salvation. The first step in getting God's attention is to accept the Son of God, the Lord Jesus, and to become a child of God.

A Prayer to Establish a Personal Relationship with God ...

Holy God, I want to know You so much, yet I know my sin has kept me from doing so. I believe You came to earth in the person of Jesus to die on the cross in my place so I could go to heaven. I now want to ask Jesus to come into my life, to forgive my sins, and to make me the kind of person You want me to be. I do not knowingly withhold any area of my life from You. Thank You for making it possible to be in a right relationship with You. Help me to know how to walk with You step by step. In Jesus's name, amen.

Step 2. The second step in getting God's attention in prayer is remembering this heavenly Father, who loves you tenderly, is also holy and to be exalted. Matthew 6:9 continues with words rarely used in today's culture: "Hallowed be your name." We don't use that word *hallowed* too much in our culture. The word springs from a root word that describes something that is set apart and significant, that is raised high above anything else you could compare it to. And when we talk about His name, we are referring to all He is and all He is about. What is His name anyway? Philippians 2:9–11 provides a glimpse into the level of exaltation deserved by our Lord: "Therefore God exalted him to the highest place and gave him the name that is above every name, that at the name of Jesus every knee should bow, in heaven and on earth and under the earth, and every tongue confess that Jesus Christ is Lord, to the glory of God the Father." Who is this high and majestic God? His name is Jesus! And when we go to prayer, we have to remember whom we're talking to. He was not just some baby whose birthday we celebrate at Christmas. He was the eternal God who came to earth to die for the sins of the world. He was God incarnate, God in the flesh. When you pray, remember, yes, He is a loving heavenly Father. But also He has a name to be worshipped and revered. Bill Hybels, pastor of the effective and innovative Willow Creek Community Church in Chicago, reminds us, "It's hard to get past the 'Our Father' in your prayer without falling back in awe at that incredible miracle. 'How great is the love the Father has lavished on us, that we should be called children of God!' (1 John 3:1)."[48]

A Prayer to Thank God for Who He Is …

Holy God, all authority and honor is Yours in heaven and on earth. Not only have You revealed to us Your majesty and holiness, but You have also reminded us we find power and comfort in Your name. You are the God who heals. You are the God who protects. You are the God who redeems. Hallowed be Your name. Amen.

Step 3. The third step in getting God's attention in prayer is remembering that our loving heavenly Father—who is holy and deserving of respect and adoration—has a weighty and significant agenda for the people on earth. In Matthew 6:10a, Jesus teaches the disciples to pray, "Your kingdom come." What's this all about? Six hundred years earlier, a man named Daniel was a prominent figure in Israel's history. Israel was under the control of the Babylonian Empire, led by a king named Nebuchadnezzar. Daniel was among some patriots of Israel who had been taken away from their homeland. It was not long before he and his cohorts assumed powerful positions in that government. In the midst of this transition, Nebuchadnezzar became convinced that the creation of *his* kingdom was the most important agenda item in the world. In fact, in Daniel 4, Nebuchadnezzar tells everyone how great he thinks he is. For seven years, he experienced a kind of insanity that drove him to live like a wild man. At the end of that time, God got his attention. He looked up and praised the God of heaven and then went on to describe God:

> "At the end of that time, I, Nebuchadnezzar, raised my eyes toward heaven, and my sanity was restored. Then I praised the Most High; I honored and glorified him who lives forever. His dominion is an eternal dominion; his kingdom endures from generation to generation. All the peoples of the earth are regarded as nothing. He does as he pleases with the powers of heaven and the peoples of the earth. No one can hold back his hand or say to him: 'What have you done?' " (Daniel 4:34–35).

Here's a guy who was about the business of building his own kingdom, and he had forgotten that he would one day leave the earth. But friends, God's kingdom is eternal. In prayer, too often we go to God with a list of what it's going to take to build *our* kingdoms. God's profound agenda is about the building of *His* kingdom by *His* people. Do you know what I find exciting about this? God's kingdom is not of this world. He's building a spiritual kingdom, and those of us who know Him are citizens of that kingdom. One day, Jesus Christ will return to this planet to restore His kingdom, and the Bible says it will never end. So when we pray, we go to God knowing not only that He's a personal God and has a powerful name, but that He has a profound agenda. Don't forget that. Don't forget in your prayers to ask God to allow you to be a part of building it.

A Prayer to Be a Part of God's Work in This World ...

Loving Lord, I can't believe You have selected me to be part of Your kingdom plan. Give me the courage to step out in faith when You call me to serve. Give me greater clarity and discernment to sense the leading of the Spirit to be your hands and feet in this dark world. And give me stamina to continue Your work through adversity and discouragement, knowing I will stand before You one day. In Jesus's name, amen.

Step 4. The fourth step to remember in getting God's attention in prayer is our loving Father, who is worthy of our worship and whose deep love for His creation has created an intense agenda for change and restoration, has a flawless plan to make these changes in and through you. Our Lord continues His instruction with "Your will be done on earth as it is in heaven" (Matthew 6:10b). What appear to be mere words of encouragement now become a bit more intimidating. Let me tell you why. First of all, it is a done deal in regards to heaven. God's will is done in heaven every day. There are no cops in heaven to police the activity. There are no newspapers in heaven because there is no bad news. In heaven, no one is trying to figure out how to get gangs and graffiti out of town. Every day in heaven is just like the day before in that God's will is done. So when you pray, you are to ask God to allow His will to be done on earth just like it's done in heaven. When you pray that, you are personalizing it. You're not saying, "Lord, let Your will be done in downtown L.A., or Bosnia, or the White House." You're praying, "Lord, let Your will be done in me." And let me tell you the implication here. One day, the Son of God made His way to one of His favorite places to pray, the Garden of Gethsemane. But this was not a bright and sunny day. It was nighttime, and He took His disciples with Him, stationed them around the garden, and told them to be on the alert. These disciples couldn't even keep themselves awake. Jesus withdrew to a private place to pray, as described for us in Matthew 26:39–42:

> Going a little farther, he fell with his face to the ground and prayed, "My Father, if it is possible, may this cup be taken from me. Yet not as I will, but as you will." Then he returned to his disciples and found them sleeping. "Could you men not keep watch with me for one hour?" he asked Peter. "Watch and pray so that you will not fall into temptation. The spirit is willing, but the body is weak." He went away a second time and prayed, "My Father, if it is not possible for this cup to be taken away unless I drink it, may your will be done."

If I could contemporize His statement, He might have said, "Father, if there's a Plan B, this would be a good time to reveal it. If there is any other way to accomplish this task for the sins of humankind, other than me experiencing this agonizing death, please show me. Nevertheless, not what I will, but what You will."

I love the words of the writer of the book of Hebrews who provides theological framing for what we are learning: "Although he was a son, he learned obedience from what he suffered and, once made perfect, he became the source of eternal salvation for all who obey him" (Hebrews 5:8–9). One of the amazing things about our Lord is that He modeled for me everything I need to live out the Christian life. And obedience was one of the most significant. The Bible says that Jesus Christ is a high priest who can identify with us because there was a moment in His life when what His flesh desired was different from what the Father wanted. But when those two ways didn't go together, He chose obedience.

A Prayer of Commitment and Submission to God ...

Father, I want to do what You show me is the right thing to do. As we both know, that is not always what happens. But I am asking You to change me, to show me how to submit to You, to reveal to me anything that is keeping me from completely yielding to Your will. Then help me do whatever is necessary to do what You want. I love You and trust You. In Jesus's name, amen.

Why Pray?

Why in the world would God open Himself to you and me in prayer? I've probably wrestled with that question a hundred times. He doesn't need to hear from me. His life goes on just fine without a call from Glen. There is never a time when God's disappointed if I don't call Him. So why would He invite us to pray? Because He loves us so much. We matter so much to God that He will listen to us at any hour—day or night.

So let me ask, how close can we draw to God and at what rate? Do you remember the story of Peter trying to walk on the water? For our Lord to be outside the boat walking on water is unacceptable to Pete—not because he is jealous but because of his earnest desire to be close to his Savior. He steps out of the boat, and as long as his eyes remain focused on Jesus, the miracle of walking on water can be checked off his "bucket list." But the moment his attention focuses on the waves of difficulties around him and the tumultuousness of the journey of life, he begins to sink. At that very moment, Peter offers the most precise prayer in the Bible, in my opinion: "Lord, save me." You need every word of that prayer for it to work. If you're going down this week, make sure you cry out to Him. Why? Because the attitude of our heart is the key to prayer. The better we know Him, the more we will trust Him, see His great capabilities, and experience His power working in and through our lives. Closeness comes as we yield ourselves to Him in trust.

But how does one go about drawing closer to God? Does it just happen over a period of time? Are there steps we can take to draw closer to God? What insights can we have? Intimacy with God is an ongoing and very necessary process. We must learn more about who God really is, what He can and will do for those He loves, what He thinks about us, and how His heart responds to us. In Jeremiah 29:11–14a, the Lord expresses these wonderful words:

> "For I know the plans I have for you," declares the LORD, "plans to prosper you and not to harm you, plans to give you hope and a future. Then you will call upon me and come and pray to me, and I will listen to you. You will seek me and find me when you seek me with all your heart. I will be found by you," declares the LORD, "and will bring you back from captivity."

As you learn these things and they sink deeply into your heart and soul, your faith and trust in Him will grow. You will want to spend time with Him, not because you ought to, but out of a heart that is awakening to the desire to spend time talking with God; a heart that is beginning to long for time with its creator as the Spirit draws you to Him; a heart that is seeking Him with all that is within it.

True Prayer Starts in the Heart of God

True prayer starts in the heart of God. He then, through the Holy Spirit, communicates this to our hearts. We feel a need to pray for what He has communicated—often even thinking that what we are praying for originated in our own hearts and minds. Then we pray this back to the Father through the name of the Lord Jesus and the right He gives us to access the Father in prayer, thus completing the circle of prayer. As the Father hears our prayer, He then answers it because we are praying according to His will. Out of this comes a wonderful by-product of this deepening understanding of God: our prayer life is richer and more meaningful. We start praying according to God's will and thus see fulfilled the promise of 1 John 5:14–15, which in essence says He not only hears us but answers our prayers if we ask anything that is according to God's will.

Answered prayer is a wonder in itself. But, as important as getting an answer is, prayer also brings joy and satisfaction as we gain a deepening knowledge of God's presence and a growing certainty that He is listening and acting on our behalf. It increases our faith and trust in Him and our courage to ask for even more that is within His will.

Because God is not visible, we can sometimes forget the wonderful friend who is there, just waiting to talk with us, to help us and to give us counsel in every aspect of our lives. Often we are preoccupied, too busy, or just negligent in going to Him. In fact, some people feel they don't want to bother the almighty God with little things such as lost keys, small financial problems, relationships, the need for a parking space, and so on.

When Should We Seek God's Help?

Here we see the first misconception: people want to use their prayers to bring only big problems to God. For some the philosophy is either "God is too busy running the universe to worry about this small problem I'm having" or "If I ask Him for this, He may not be willing to help me when I really need it. So I'll solve this one myself and run to Him when it is something more important." To such people, it is as though they have only a certain number of "chips" with God, and they must be wise in the way they spend them, lest they run out and not have any when they really need Him.

For many, life has convinced them they are not worth very much, so they conclude God will not be interested in helping them. They feel insignificant and unworthy, so they wonder, "Why pray?" To others, past sin makes them feel unworthy of God's help. Then there are those who have been discouraged in the past when God has said no and have given up on asking God, lest they be disappointed again. Such disappointment reinforced their already strong feelings of rejection, alienation, and poor self-image.

Trust and commitment are very difficult when we have any of these misconceptions about God. Satan is the source and wants us to remain unenlightened about how wonderful and satisfying a deep, trusting relationship with God is. If Satan weakens our faith, then he can greatly neutralize our effectiveness for the Lord.

On the other hand, many people have very self-centered motives for prayer and for spending time with God. They use Him as a "store" to which they bring their shopping list, expecting it to be filled. Often this is because they feel they have earned God's favor by doing good things for Him and His people. Therefore, God "owes" it to them to answer their prayers.

Others feel they are so needy that God is obligated to help them even though they may be doing little in the relationship. It is basically a one-way street where God is the one to give and they are the ones to receive. They neither spend much time in worship nor talk to their loving friend. They don't feel the need to do so. "He will understand," they say. "Anyway, He's probably too busy or not interested in what I have to say. Not only that, He already knows all about me, so why bother to tell Him what He already knows?"

Their relationship with God is never strengthened, and they go sadly through life with a distorted picture of God because they have never taken the time to seek Him, to develop a desire for Him, or to get to know this awesome God who has reached out to them in love. Like Eve, they have been willing to buy whatever lie is given them about God and their relationship to Him. They have ignored the true picture of God revealed in the pages of Scripture, painted in all of nature and written in their own hearts.

As in so many other ways, Jesus is a wonderful example of the relationship we can have with God. He had such a close relationship with the Father because He was both God and man, and so He knew He had to spend time with the Father, talking with Him, seeking His face, His will, and His blessings.

What Is the Key to Our Relationship with God?

Having set the example, Jesus then demonstrated the key to His human relationships. Two words usually overlooked in Mark 3:14 reveal the key. We read that when Jesus appointed the twelve apostles, they were to be "with Him." Wow! To be with Jesus twenty-four hours a day! Wouldn't that be wonderful? To watch Him minister, to hear His teachings, to walk with Him, to see Him in unguarded moments, to be discipled and trained by Him. Who wouldn't want that? And yet we have something even better—the Father, the Spirit, *and* Jesus living inside us—in constant communication with us, if we will only listen.

Your loving heavenly Father is waiting to hear from you. As our exalted God, His name is powerful and trustworthy. His agenda goes far beyond the initiation of a movement and the limited and pointless plans of man. He is going to use you and me to redeem this world—one life at a time. Don't miss out on the greatest of all joys, knowing Jesus personally and talking to Him intimately and honestly in prayer.

Questions to Ponder and Discuss

1. What are the common excuses people use for not praying, and what are they really saying? Which one(s) have you used?

2. Read Ephesians 6:18–20 and James 5:16–18: How do your prayers contribute to the spiritual battle you face on your journey of life?

3. What are the strengths and weaknesses of your prayer life?

4. Who has modeled an effective prayer life to you? What qualities do you want to imitate?

5. In one sentence, summarize what needs to change in your life for prayer to become more of a priority.

Recommended Reading

Prayer: Finding the Heart's True Home by Richard Foster
Prayer: Does It Make Any Difference? by Philip Yancey
The Ministry of Intercession: A Plea for More Prayer by Andrew Murray

The Journey Continues ... Now, better armed through prayer and an improved worship experience, we are ready to deal with some of the harder pathways God places before us. The next two chapters will examine the issues of God's calling, your vocation, and the trials and pain of life. You will discover God is more interested in your character than He is in your comfort. You will find God will often use your career to shape you into His servant. Let's continue the journey into a season of work.

9

Career and Calling:
Discerning God's Plan for Your Vocation

Greg Piken

*Christians with a thankful heart
experience more joy in their work and
better reflect to others that they have a
relationship with a God who has blessed them.*

As the young-adult pastor at Journey of Faith, I generally work with two very different types of people. I see energized college students ready to shape and conquer the world for the glory of God. And I see the post-college crowd asking, "What happened to me?" Some who have recently completed college spend a great deal of time looking for their dream job but cannot find it. Others quickly panic after graduation and take a well-paying occupation that drains the life out of them. In both cases, the results are the same: they are less excited about life and forget the big dreams they had when they were passionate college students.

For many, this comes from frustration and the assumption that God is somehow silent on the issue of what He wants from their lives. I often hear people say that they are waiting for God's direction for their career or ministry. Usually, they have no idea what they mean when they say that. A few people seem to expect an angel to descend from heaven, fly into their bedroom in the middle of the night, and hand them an outline mapping out the rest of their lives!

We read stories of the Old Testament patriarchs and prophets—stories in which God shows up in burning bushes, thunderstorms, and apocalyptic visions—and we suppose that God will show us His will for our lives in much the same way. It's important to recognize that although God is certainly capable of showing up and communicating any way He pleases, these events are recorded in Scripture because they are so unique and special. God had a specific task for a specific person at a specific time.

So what about the rest of us? If God doesn't clearly communicate out of the clouds to us, how are we to know what to do with our lives? Whether you have not yet decided on a career or are well into your work life, I believe God gives His people a number of ways to know and own their callings.

The Role of Faith

When I was eighteen years old, I was going to be a famous actor. At twenty-two, I was going to be a famous recording artist. The twenty-six-year-old Greg was set on becoming a worship pastor. Now, at the age of thirty, I've found my calling as the young-adult and local outreach pastor at Journey of Faith. At no point along the way did I have one of the aforementioned "burning bush" moments, but I did have a sense of how God was working in my life and what He was doing around me. I knew that I absolutely loved being around people all the time. I knew that I had the ability to encourage and motivate people in their faith and personal goals. Over the years, I have taken steps toward improving those abilities and finding better ways to use them. An angel from heaven didn't tell me to go to seminary. It was by faith I decided to learn and equip myself better. I didn't have a dream that I would someday be a pastor, but by faith, I knew that God had given me abilities that were best used in that role. I also looked around and saw a church, community, and world that I was passionate about reaching. I desperately wanted to see God's people take an active role in sharing the gospel, mentoring children and youth, and caring for the poor, hungry, and marginalized. By faith, I knew that as a pastor, I would be able to play that role.

Although I recognize that everyone has a different story, my hope is that you recognize that God sometimes asks you to take a step of faith—a step that you must sometimes take without seeing where your foot will land. Hebrews 11:1 says that "faith is being sure of what we hope for and certain of what we do not see." If we always knew clearly what God was doing, we wouldn't need much faith in order to follow. God calls us to trust His plan and to "live by faith, not by sight" (2 Corinthians 5:7).

God's General Will

The most important thing we need to know is that what God communicates to us about our calling will never contradict what He says in His Word, the Bible. I have heard people share that what they feel has been a vision from God, and the first thing I ask them is whether or not it lines up with Scripture. As an extreme example, I've heard people tell me they connect with God when they take illegal drugs or when they have extramarital sex. In both cases, I assured them it was not God to whom they were connecting. No matter what they claimed to have felt, it was not God's will, because God never condones such behavior in His Word. Some acts are less black and white, however, so it's helpful to use what I call "the filters." God gave all His followers some very big-picture instructions about what He most wanted to see from His people.

Filter 1: Do everything for God's glory! The apostle Paul tells us in 1 Corinthians 10:31, "whether you eat or drink or whatever you do, do it all for the glory of God." This passage comes at the conclusion of a section in which Paul tells members of the early church that they need to stop thinking of their freedom in Christ as a license to seek pleasure, but rather as an opportunity to be a light to others. He adds two verses later, "I am not seeking my own good but the good of many, so that they may be saved." As we then examine our own lives and callings, we need to use Filter 1—the filter of God's glory. Ask yourself if the career or ministry you are pursuing is being done for God's glory or your own. Will this job help you be a light to others? Will the money you make be used for God's glory or simply for your own benefit? Is the position you are seeking going to be used to make God's name known, or just your own name? Filter 1 is a chance for you to ask if what you are doing is really going to honor God. I think most of us have some idea as soon as we hear about a career or ministry opportunity.

Erick is a personal trainer who asked himself these questions. Over the years, he became passionate about helping the homeless, so he decided to use his workplace to do that. For one month, he offered three free personal training sessions to the gym member who brought in the most toiletry items for the homeless. The response was incredible! His clients started bringing in more toiletries than would fit in the boxes he provided. Soon, he was connected with a major toothpaste company that provided carloads of free hygiene kits. He was also able to have great conversations with coworkers and gym members about how God was moving in his life. Erick found a way to glorify God in his job, and his work was immensely satisfying as a result.

Filter 2: Love God and love people! Jesus says in Matthew 22:37–40, " 'Love the Lord your God with all your heart and with all your soul and with all your mind.' This is the first and greatest commandment. And the second is like it: 'Love your neighbor as yourself.' All the law and the prophets hang on these two commandments." Jesus presents us with Filter 2—the filter of love. This is when we need to take our career and ministry callings and ask if what we are doing will directly or indirectly help us or others to love God and people. If not, will it give us future opportunities to love God and others?

Dave is a car salesman but is known by his coworkers as more of a counselor. Whenever I catch up with him, he is asking me to pray for someone at the dealership. Dave often invites his coworkers over for dinner and takes the opportunity to ask them about their personal lives. Simply by lovingly listening and talking, Dave has helped one coworker restore his broken marriage, another decide against having an abortion, and a third decide to start going to church with him. Dave realizes that he has a powerful ministry at the car dealership because he knows it's God's will for him to love others.

Filter 3: Make disciples! Before ascending to heaven, Jesus left His followers with clear instructions to " 'go and make disciples of all nations, baptizing them in the name of the Father and of the Son and of the Holy Spirit, and teaching them to obey everything I have commanded you' " (Matthew 28:19–20a). In other words, Jesus left us with Filter 3—the filter of disciple making.

Although spiritual gifts apply specifically to your role in building up the body of Christ, I believe we can apply this concept to our careers as well.

Jason owns a film production company and shoots commercials for several high-level companies. Although he loves his profession, he's passionate about meeting new people with whom he can share the gospel. His strongest desire is to make each film shoot an opportunity to connect with someone and share the hope he has in Jesus Christ. He sets his work through Filter 3 and goes out into the film world to win new disciples.

Knowing that God has clearly called each of us to glorify Him, to love Him and others, and to make disciples should give us all an enormous sense of purpose no matter where we end up in our careers and ministries. As you ponder God's calling for your life, you must weigh what you think your calling may be against Scripture and run the opportunities God gives you through these three filters.

How God Made You

Even though God has a general will that applies to all of us, I believe that He gives us each a unique role to play within His purpose. A verse that has forever shaped my thinking of God's call on my life comes from Ephesians 2:10. "For we are God's workmanship, created in Christ Jesus to do good works, which God prepared in advance for us to do." What this verse tells us is radically important. Before we were even born, we were shaped by the God of the universe for a unique and special purpose that comes from His own heart and plan. What could give us a greater sense of purpose and motivation? Scripture shows us that we can and should pursue the discovery of our individual callings through the use of our spiritual gifts.

The apostle Paul makes clear that God gives each Christian at least one spiritual gift. "Now to each one the manifestation of the Spirit is given for the common good" (1 Corinthians 12:7). Wayne Grudem, well-respected author, professor, and theologian, defines a spiritual gift as "any ability that is empowered by the Holy Spirit and used in any ministry of the church."[49] Some of the spiritual gifts listed in Scripture—particularly Romans 12, 1 Corinthians 12, and Ephesians 4—include administration, discernment, encouragement, evangelism, faith, giving, hospitality, knowledge, leadership, mercy, pastoring or shepherding, prophecy, service or help, teaching, and wisdom. God wants to gift us and create us specifically so that we can be a blessing to others.

Although spiritual gifts apply specifically to your role in building up the body of Christ, I believe we can apply this concept to our careers as well. God created you uniquely, and that means you will naturally interact with people differently from others, find different subject matter more interesting, and have abilities and inabilities that set you apart.

Alec has the gift of discernment, and as a police officer, he is able to recognize people who could pose a threat almost instantly. Stephanie has the gift of knowledge and is fascinated by the research she does as a hospital blood analyst. Jasmine has the gift of hospitality and works at a lounge at the Los Angeles International Airport where she is able to help weary pilots, flight attendants, and travelers relax. Start consciously thinking and writing out those environments, topics, and skills that energize or excite you, and let that guide your decision-making process. When you do what

God has created you to do, you will be happier and far more productive for the kingdom of God.

Knowing God Means Knowing His Will

I can honestly say that the people I know who have had the most clarity about God's leadership in their own lives are people who are passionately in love with God's Word. The more we get to know God through His Word, the more we understand how He actually thinks. I believe this is what the apostle Paul meant when he said that we have "the mind of Christ" (1 Corinthians 2:16).

My friend Brent knows me very well. He knows how I am likely to respond to stress. He can read my facial expressions and translate what they mean, and he generally knows what to say and when I need to hear it. This did not happen overnight. We have been friends for several years, we are in the ministry together, we're roommates, and we hang out with the same circle of friends. He's come to know me very well through a variety of situations.

We need to view our relationships with God in the same way. By reading His Word, we can see how God has responded to people over thousands of years. We can see His love, patience, justice, wrath, faithfulness, holiness, and so on through His dealings with humankind. The more we study His Word, the more we will come to know how He would respond to the decisions we face in life. Then we can say with increasing certainty that we can better know God's will for our lives.

Praying for God's Will

Prayer, as we were reminded in the last chapter, is an integral part of seeking God's will. I'm often asked how to pray specifically for a calling. Many prayers of great believers are recorded in the Bible, and they can help to strengthen our language of prayer. In addition to asking for specific direction, these prayers also express a desire to get to know God Himself better. Note how Paul prays for the church in Ephesus, "I keep asking that the God of our Lord Jesus Christ, the glorious Father, may give you the Spirit of wisdom and revelation, so that you may know him better"

(Ephesians 1:17). Maturing in the Christian life seems intimately connected with praying for God's will. Paul shares this observation in regard to the prayer life of Epaphras, a leader in the Colossian church. "Epaphras, who is one of you and a servant of Christ Jesus, sends greetings. He is always wrestling in prayer for you, that you may stand firm in all the will of God, mature and fully assured" (Colossians 4:12). Thus, as you pray for God's will for your life, don't just ask God for a job. Make sure it is God Himself whom you desire to know and please.

Look for Where God Is Already Working

In Acts 16, Paul, Silas, and Timothy have their hearts set on going to Asia, but God clearly guides them in the opposite direction toward Europe. God had already been working on the hearts of the people there to open them to the message of the gospel. Never forget that the Holy Spirit is already at work in the lives of your coworkers and clients before you even think to apply for the job. Too often, we make our own decisions and *then* ask God to "bless" them. Be sure to pray and ask God ahead of time how He is already working, and what you can do to help.

Seek Advice

As you ponder some of life's biggest decisions, and this is certainly one of them, you should never underestimate the importance of seeking wise godly counsel. "For lack of guidance a nation falls, but many advisers make victory sure" (Proverbs 11:14). 1 Kings 12 documents very little of the life of King Solomon's son, Rehoboam, except for a very poor decision he made. His subjects were crying out for tax relief. Although his godly older advisers encouraged him to provide assistance for his kingdom, his younger friends gave him bad advice and told him to raise taxes instead. As a result, both God and his people were unhappy with the king, and all but one of the tribes of Israel broke away from his kingdom. Bad advice led to a tragic division among God's people. The psalmist reminds us that "blessed is the man who does not walk in the counsel of the wicked, or stand in the way of sinners, or sit in the seat of mockers. But his delight is in the law of the LORD, and on his law he meditates day and night" (Psalm 1:1–2). Talk to people whom you respect—people who will be coming from a godly point of view. Talk to a Christian who knows you well and can help you apply God's Word to your life. Perhaps that is a pastor, a Bible study leader, a mentor, a friend, a family member, or a coworker whom you trust. It helps that they know you so that they can pray for you, remind you of God's "filters," and help you take inventory of your spiritual gifts and life circumstances. I also recommend taking the time to see a career counselor. Many churches and Bible colleges offer classes or appointments with professionals who are skilled at helping people discover the careers for which they are best suited.

Attitude on the Job

It's fun to think "big picture" about the future and romanticize about how God will use us later in life. We can't forget, though, that God has given us today to live out His will. It's important that we remember to be Christians in the environment where God has us now, even if we want out. There are five ways that you can biblically rethink your current job situation by your attitude and ethics.

1. Find purpose and excellence in what you do. If you approach your job without thinking through the value of your work, it will become too easy to feel defeated or meaningless. Your job exists because there is a need for it. Pastor and author Bill Hybels eloquently frames this idea in his book *Christians in the Marketplace.* He says, "Dignity is available to every person in every legitimate, worthwhile profession. The farmer who plows a straight furrow, the accountant whose books balance, the truck driver who backs his 40-foot rig into a narrow loading dock, the teacher who delivers a well-prepared lesson, the carpenter who keeps the building square, the executive who reads the market accurately … the secretary who types the perfect page … all experience dignity as they commit themselves to their labors."[50] When you undertake a task or project, work to the best of your abilities. When you complete an assignment, take a minute to appreciate the value of your work.

2. Respect your boss and coworkers. This is difficult for a lot of people because they feel that their bosses and coworkers are not worthy of their respect. Remember that it is God's job, not ours, to assign value to people. In fact, Philippians 2:3 reminds us to "Do nothing out of selfish ambition or vain conceit, but in humility consider others better than yourselves." Imagine how differently we'd see our jobs if we started viewing people as better than ourselves or as they are: men and women created in the image of God. We also are called to be the kind of coworker anyone would want to have, and we can achieve this calling by respecting and seeing worth in others. You can accomplish this by being on time and helping associates without being asked. Also, don't be lazy, but "Whatever you do, work at it with all your heart, as working for the Lord, not for men" (Colossians 3:23).

3. Be an encourager. This can be far more difficult than it sounds in workplaces where gossip, cursing, and tearing people down are part of the culture. Colossians 3:8 warns us to "rid yourselves of all things such as these: anger, rage, malice, slander, and filthy language from your lips." The apostle Paul goes on to explain that as believers who have put on a "new self" (Colossians 3:10) we should speak differently than the rest of the world because we're being renewed in the image of our Creator. This means speaking well of others, being kind to coworkers regardless of how they act toward you, and thanking them when they support you. I also find that when I stop and genuinely pray for a coworker, it becomes far easier to love them afterward.

4. Be grateful. Philippians 2:14 cautions us to "do everything without complaining or arguing." In an economy where many struggle to find work, remember to be thankful for what God has given you. Christians with a thankful heart experience more joy in their work and better reflect to others that they have a relationship with a God who has blessed them.

5. Be ethical. Our society celebrates success and power, which makes it tempting to lie or cheat to climb the corporate ladder. Large mortgage payments, bills, and the cost of raising families only increase the pressure to cut corners. Jesus gives us a poignant reminder that unethically pursuing ambition or achieving success will lead to destruction. In Matthew 16:26, He asks, " 'What good will it be for a man if he gains the whole world, yet forfeits his soul? Or what can a man give in exchange for his soul?' " By reminding us of His own worth, God encourages believers to overcome the temptations to lie, cheat, or act unethically to achieve money or success. Scripture compares our relationship with God to treasure (Matthew 13:44) and claims that our faith is of more worth than gold (1 Peter 1:7). When you value your relationship with God over your career, He promises to be faithful and provide for your needs. " 'Seek first his kingdom and his righteousness, and all these things will be given to you as well' " (Matthew 6:33).

Words of Encouragement

Working for the glory of God can be simultaneously frustrating and exhilarating. Some people try a number of jobs along the way before they find their best possible fit. Others can't find the work to which they're best suited because of a competitive job market, a difficult economy, or the inability to move to another town or city. Never forget that you are in God's hands during this whole process. Sometimes, He uses temporary jobs, imperfect coworkers, and confusing life decisions to grow us in our faith or to accomplish something we would never otherwise expect. Don't lose faith. Know that when God calls you, it's for a reason! Make sure to discern between "being realistic" and "being complacent" when it comes to having great faith on the job. Far too many Christians settle for the status quo rather than pursue the great callings that God has for their careers. Keep seeking God with all your heart, mind, and soul, and remember Paul's words in Ephesians 4:1, "I urge you to live a life worthy of the calling you have received."

Questions to Ponder and Discuss

1. Read Romans 12, 1 Corinthians 12, and Ephesians 4:1–13. How do you think God has gifted you, and how could that apply to your career?

2. Does anyone come to you for help or advice in a specific field? How could that apply to your calling?

3. Do you ever feel like you might be scared to know God's will? Would following God's will mean making hard decisions or sacrifices in your life?

4. Have you ever struggled to find purpose in your work? How can you use the three "filters" to make your job more meaningful?

5. Does your current work environment lead to temptation to be dishonest, impure, or unethical? What are some proactive steps you can take to be Christ-like on the job?

Recommended Reading

Business as a Calling by Michael Novak

Living Your Strengths by Albert Winsemen, Donald O. Clifton, and Curt Liesveld

Next Generation Leader: 5 Essentials for Those Who Will Shape the Future by Andy Stanley

The Journey Continues … Aren't you just a bit surprised at what God has to say about your job? We hope you have a better understanding about the holiness of your vocation in God's eyes. Now we will study the trials we experience in life. One of the great things about reading the Bible is knowing God doesn't pull any punches when telling us the truth and backing this truth with examples. Trials are one of those areas. You are about to be educated and equipped for the times when God leads you into a season of trial.

10

Trials:
Singing a Song of Faith During Crisis

Jason Cusick

*In the trials we face, may our laments
show the same honesty and faithfulness as our Lord's.*

"What else is going to happen?"

He looked out over the empty fields. They had once been filled with cattle and sheep tended by a large crew of hired help. The sights and sounds of herds and flocks spread across his acres of property had made him believe there would always be food on the table and money for whatever needs arose. Now the fields were empty, and he was bankrupt.

He turned to the northern corner of his property, glancing at what used to be the home of his oldest son. In the place where his large family used to celebrate God's abundance, there was only silence. The strong walls were now just a pile of rubble. The debris had not been moved since the storm. His family was gone.

He wanted to cry, but it was too painful. The salt from his tears caused the sores on his face to sting. Moving was difficult as well. The blisters were everywhere, and he had scratched himself raw looking for some relief. He had done all he could to avoid behaviors and habits that lead to chronic illness, but now his health was gone.

He collapsed to the ground. He had done his best to live the right way. Why was this happening?

This story, a brief summary of trials explored in the book of Job, is not that different from the trials we face today. Financial ruin. Grief. Illness. Loneliness. Spiritual exhaustion. We all have, and will, experience trials in our lives. Some will be expected; others will take us by surprise. How we respond will determine how well we will endure and overcome what comes our way.

Unhelpful Responses to Trials

What do we do when the unexpected trials hit? It could be the death of a loved one, job loss, depression, bankruptcy, infidelity, an arrest, a lawsuit, or a health crisis. Sometimes the crisis is about one's identity, guilt from sin, or a loss of faith. Many of us have heard the overly simplistic or even erroneous responses to unexpected trials ...

"Look on the bright side of things."
"God will never give you more than you can bear."
"Time heals all wounds."

"You will be stronger after you get through this."

"God works everything for the good."

"You can always have another child."

Most of these things are said with a genuine desire to help, but they fall short of helping us in the way we need. In the book of Job, Job's friends come to help him but offer all the wrong kinds of support. In their day, suffering was always seen as a consequence of sin. If your flocks were killed by invading armies, it was because God was judging you. If your family was killed by a natural disaster, it was because they were living an immoral life. If you developed painful boils on your body, it was because you were engaged in some secret sin that needed to be confessed. Job's friends decided the best approach to comforting their friend was to pry a confession out of him! (See Job 5:1–17, 8:1–10, 11:1–6.) In Job's situation, sin had nothing to do with suffering. He called out for compassionate support:

> "I have heard many things like these; miserable comforters are you all! Will your long-winded speeches never end? What ails you that you keep on arguing? I also could speak like you, if you were in my place; I could make fine speeches against you and shake my head at you. But my mouth would encourage you; comfort from my lips would bring you relief" (Job 16:2–5).

When we are going through trials, what we need is loving support, practical help, and someone who isn't afraid to feel the painful feelings we are having. We don't need clichés or well-crafted theological responses. We need to cry, shout, be confused, ask the tough questions, and sit in the silence when God doesn't seem to be responding. The Bible does not tell us to "help sad people be happy" or "stop the tears of hurting people." The Bible says, "mourn with those who mourn" (Romans 12:15). How do we do this? What help does the Bible give us when we face unexpected trials?

A Song for Suffering

Do you have a favorite song? People have favorite songs for different reasons. Maybe it was playing during a special time in your life or it has a great sound that makes you feel a certain way. Favorite songs often say what we want to say, but they do it better. We play them so they will speak for us. We play them so they can help us express how we feel.

The Bible has its own songbook—the Psalms. It is filled with songs of thanksgiving, praise, and celebration. But it also contains songs for times of suffering. Those songs are called "lament psalms" or "complaint psalms." The Bible contains many laments, including Psalm 12, 22, 44, and 77. The book of Lamentations is a lament. Some Bible scholars have suggested that the entire book of Job is a biblical lament written as a drama.

Laments are the songs sung by God's people when the painful trials arrive. I believe that these songs can serve as a guide for how to talk, feel, and act when we face suffering in our lives. Below are six common elements of lament psalms, which I have rewritten as guidelines for what to do when facing a trial.

1. Lay Out the Problem

Susan was struggling in her relationship with her boyfriend. He was mean and controlling. She worked hard to try to communicate to him what she was feeling and thinking, but the problems were only getting worse.

> "I don't know what to do," she told her friend. "He doesn't respect me."
> "Is that the problem?" her friend asked.
> "I think so," she replied. "I need him to change."
> "Why?" her friend asked.
> "Because I love him," she quickly answered.
> "I don't understand. He's treated you this way for two years. He hasn't changed yet."
> "If he respected me, he wouldn't allow himself to be mean to me," Susan reasoned.
> "But you're allowing it," her friend replied.
> "Are you saying I'm the problem?" Susan said defensively.

Sometimes what (or who) we think is the problem isn't the problem. Discovering the problem is the first step. It is also one of the most difficult parts of suffering because we often misdiagnose the problem. The problem may be in us or someone else. The problem may have specific spiritual origins or be something very natural. The Bible points us to five possible origins of suffering.

Cause and Effect: This is the natural order of the world, otherwise known as cause and effect. For example, you stub your toe; it gets a bruise. Some would include natural disasters in this category.

Consequences for Sin: This is a spiritual form of cause and effect or "reaping and sowing." (See Galatians 6:7.)

Divine Training: This is when God specifically causes a problem in one's life for the purpose of spiritual growth and challenge. This can also include when God corrects sin. (See Hebrews 12:7–11.)

Spiritual Attack: This is when Satan is allowed to bring suffering into one's life. It is important to remember that God is not removed or powerless during these attacks. (See Ephesians 6:10–18.)

Mystery: This is when we are suffering and despite our discernment and counsel, do not understand why. It does not mean that our suffering is meaningless or random—but that given our limited understanding, we do not know the cause.

Laying out the problem may take time. It also helps to have some patient and thoughtful people to help ask you questions. Deciding on the problem too quickly will cause you to look to the wrong places for solutions. You'll blame others when you should be looking to yourself, or you'll accuse yourself when you don't need to. Many people look for solutions to the problems of their soul by changing things on the outside. They quit their job, move to another city, get a divorce, change churches, or try to change something within their church, rather than looking inside and asking God about themselves. *What is the "real" problem you are facing?*

2. Allow for Your Emotions

The psalmist writes, "I cried out to God for help; I cried out to God to hear me. When I was in distress, I sought the Lord; at night I stretched out untiring hands and my soul refused to be comforted. I remembered you, O God, and I groaned; I mused, and my spirit grew faint" (Psalm 77:1–3).

Many religious people are uncomfortable about feelings. They carry the belief that if their thinking is correct, their feelings will follow in an orderly fashion. But feelings don't work like that. They are messy. They can't be boxed in. They need to be expressed.

Nancy Guthrie, whose infant daughter died of a metabolic disorder, describes her struggle to share her feelings with other Christians:

> It's only natural that people around me often ask searchingly, "How are you?" And for much of the first year after Hope's death, my answer was, "I'm deeply and profoundly sad." ... Our culture wants to put the Band-Aid of heaven on the hurt of losing someone we love. Sometimes it seems like the people around us think that because we know the one we love is in heaven, that we shouldn't feel sad. But they don't understand how far away heaven feels, and how long the future seems as we see before us the years we have to spend on earth before we see the one we love again. The day after we buried Hope, I understood for the first time why so many people choose to medicate their pain in so many harmful ways. That day I tried to sleep it away. And in the days that followed, I discovered that I could not sleep it away, shop it away, eat it away, drink it away, or travel it away. ... I realized that I had a choice—I could try to stuff the hurt away in a closet, pretend it wasn't there, and wish it would disappear, or I could bring it out into the open, expose it to the Light, probe it, accept it, and allow it to heal. ... That's what Job did. Out of the deepest agony and pain from loss, Job openly mourned. He didn't cover up his sadness or put on a happy face or offer religious-sounding clichés. He tore his robe and shaved his head. He hurt. And he was not ashamed to show how deeply he hurt.[51]

Instead of stuffing, numbing, or hiding our feelings behind good theology, we need to express what we are feeling. Job was bold in declaring,

" 'Therefore I will not keep silent; I will speak out in the anguish of my spirit, I will complain in the bitterness of my soul' " (Job 7:11).

Sometimes there are cultural barriers to expressing feelings. Some families admire stoicism and cold logic when they are suffering. But God has designed us as feeling, as well as thinking, beings! All the great spiritual giants of Scripture expressed deep feelings during their trying times (Genesis 37:33–35, 1 Samuel 12:15–23, 1 Kings 19:3–5, John 11:35, Acts 20:37–38). We can follow their example.

I believe many people have problems expressing feelings because they have a limited vocabulary for emotions. This is often common with men. Consider the following list of feeling words. Is your list longer or shorter than this list?

happy	sad	fearful	playful
content	depressed	hesitant	frisky
pleased	disinterested	anxious	intrigued
excited	disappointed	restless	curious
satisfied	discouraged	doubtful	liberated

We should not be completely dominated by our feelings, because if we were, we would not be able to think and process our thoughts. But refraining from emotion will cause great damage. Many people suffer physical problems because they have no healthy outlet for expressing their feelings. A biblical lament involves pouring out our feelings to God and to those we trust. *What are you feeling?*

3. Make Your Request

"I want the pain to stop."
"I want to feel happy again."
"I want enough money to make ends meet."
"I want to be able to forgive."

Many people approach prayer like magic. They believe that if they ask for the right thing in the right way, they will get it. Laments are not secret formulas for getting what you want. They are a way for you to express your heart to God. This means that part of a lament is asking for what you would like to see happen.

The psalmist asked for healing, salvation, and rescue from his enemies (Psalm 22:19). Job wanted several things: an answer, to plead his case (13:3, 17–22), relief from pain (6:8-10), consolation, and heavenly mediation (9:32–35). When people came to Jesus, He would ask them, "What do you want from me?" Many times we don't know what we want. If we knew what we wanted, it might help us get out of suffering—or get through it more effectively.

I look at "Making Your Request" as the most experimental part of a lament. As we verbalize a request, we question it, revise it, and put disclaimers on it. There is something about saying what we want and hearing ourselves say it that helps us get more clarity. Consider the following example:

"Things are bad right now. God, please let me win the lottery. I mean, I don't want the lottery. What I want is enough money to not worry. I don't know how much that would be. I guess I'd be worried about money even if I had a lot. But a million dollars would be good. Yes, a million. Of course, a couple hundred thousand would get me out of this hole and give me some breathing room. I guess what I really want is to be able to breathe again. If I could make the payments on time, that's the big deal. I don't want to sink further. If I had what I needed to keep living the way I am living now. I know there are some changes that need to be made. I've been sitting on that stuff that I could sell, so I guess there are some things I could do. I can live more simply. God, I guess I need the kick in the pants to change some things in my life, and then the patience to trust You for my monthly payments."

When we make our request to God, we don't have to be perfect. When you pray and ask God for something, He doesn't say, "Okay, you asked for it. No changing your mind!" When we lament, we tell God what we want in unfinished form, and through our lament, He helps us refine our desires. As we pray and seek God's direction, He helps us check our motives and assists us in seeing a much bigger picture. *What would you like to see happen?*

4. Examine Yourself

In the lament psalms, the writer eventually does one of two things: he confesses the sin that has led to the suffering or makes a vow of innocence. Consider the following passages:

> For I know my transgressions, and my sin is always before me. Against you, you only, have I sinned and done what is evil in your sight, so you are proved right when you speak and justified when you judge (Psalm 51:3–4).

> "But he knows the way that I take; when he has tested me, I will come forth as gold. My feet have closely followed his steps; I have kept to his way without turning aside. I have not departed from the commands of his lips; I have treasured the words of his mouth more than my daily bread" (Job 23:10–12).

In Psalm 51, David knows that his suffering has resulted from his sin. In lamenting to God, he makes sure he confesses what he has done wrong. Conversely, Job has examined himself and sees no connection between his suffering and his lifestyle. He knows he is suffering, but it is not because of his sin.

Laments are the songs sung by God's people when the painful trials arrive. I believe that these songs can serve as a guide for how to talk, feel and act when we face suffering in our lives.

Though suffering is not always because of sin, we do need to examine ourselves. Taking inventory of our lives is an important part of getting through our trials. But this should be done in the right way. Some people are too heavy-handed with themselves and others. They see sin and guilt behind every pain in life. If sin cannot be found, they assume there is a secret unconfessed sin lurking behind the scenes. Other people are prideful and narcissistic. They are quick to declare their innocence and regularly present themselves as the victims of other people's sins. Most of us would probably place ourselves firmly in the middle of these extremes, but our times of unexpected trials may naturally push us toward one extreme or the other.

Examining ourselves is important because Scripture teaches that suffering is one of God's vehicles for developing our character:

> Not only so, but we also rejoice in our sufferings, because we know that suffering produces perseverance; perseverance, character; and character, hope. And hope does not disappoint us, because God has poured out his love into our hearts by the Holy Spirit, whom he has given us (Romans 5:3–5).

We may not be rejoicing that the stock market crashed, our family member died, the cancer returned, or our child has relapsed. But we can embrace the knowledge that God will use what is happening to us to help us grow, deepen our faith, and eventually minister to others (2 Corinthians 1:3–4). We can't fast-forward this step. We may want to ask, "What are You teaching me, Lord?" in the belief that the suffering will end once we have heard what God wants. But this is not how God works. God wants us to continually examine our lives, confess the ways we have failed to follow Him, and celebrate the ways we have remained faithful.

This part of the lament is a "turning point." It will determine the direction of your heart and your action plan for dealing with your suffering. *What are you learning about yourself?*

5. Note God's Past Work

After an extended tear-filled lament, Asaph comes to the following conclusion: "Then I thought, 'To this I will appeal: the years of the right hand of the Most High.' I will remember the deeds of the LORD; yes, I will remember your miracles of long ago. I will meditate on all your works and consider all your mighty deeds" (Psalm 77:10–12).

Why do we go to church and Bible studies? Why do we read and reread the same ancient book? It is not so we will discover some new hidden truth that no one has ever known. It is not so we can find some encrypted message about our future. We come together and explore God's Word to remind ourselves of who God is and how He has worked in the past.

We need to be reminded.

The historical books of the Bible record God's work among the patriarchs and the Israelites. The Psalms are filled with lengthy praises of how God has worked throughout history among people. The prophets state God's promises and fulfillment of those promises. We need Scripture to know how God has worked in the past. This gives us an idea of how He might work in our trials. Here we find promises and assurances:

> He gives strength to the weary and increases the power of the weak ... those who hope in the LORD will renew their strength (Isaiah 40:29, 31).

> The LORD is close to the brokenhearted and saves those who are crushed in spirit (Psalm 34:18).

> "Blessed are those who mourn, for they will be comforted" (Matthew 5:4).

The Bible is not the only place where we can learn about God's work. We can also listen to the older saints we know and get their stories. One of my favorite psalms is Psalm 44. Verse 1 reads, "We have heard with our ears, O God; our fathers have told us what you did in their days, in days long ago." This verse reminds me to listen when the older saints I know talk about what God has done in their lives. I enjoy having older adults tell me how God guided them in their lives and the lessons they have learned.

We can also note God's past work in our own lives. This comes through what is called "spiritual autobiography." A spiritual autobiography is the story of how God has worked in your life as far back as you can remember: It's the story of God and you. When we take the time to think about how God has worked in our lives, we can notice patterns, cycles, and moments of insight. They do not make the future predictable. But being aware of how God has worked in your life in the past can help you get a sense of how God may work in the future.

When we are going through a trial, we want to know where God is and what God is doing. Noting how God has worked in the past can give us confidence and hope in finding God in the present—and the future. *How has God worked previously (among His people and in your life)?*

6. Thank and Trust God

The final element common in lament psalms is thanksgiving. Thanksgiving is an important characteristic of Christians. Believers thank God in advance for what will happen. This is what "faith" is all about. "Now faith is being sure of what we hope for and certain of what we do not see. This is what the ancients were commended for" (Hebrews 11:1–2).

As part of a "lament" or "complaint," we should also consider our expectation of the future. After the problem has been explored, feelings have been expressed, requests have been made, sin has been confessed, faithfulness has been celebrated, and God's past work has been considered, there remains only one more thing to do—thank God for what God has done, is doing, and will do.

In Psalm 22 David pours out his lament and concludes by looking forward to giving his testimony to other believers, saying, "I will declare your name to my brothers; in the congregation I will praise you" (Psalm 22:22). He doesn't just look for the end of his trial but praises God for the end of everyone else's trials as well:

All the ends of the earth will remember and turn to the LORD, and all the families of the nations will bow down before him, for dominion belongs to the LORD and he rules over the nations. All the rich of the earth will feast and worship; all who go down to the dust will kneel before him—those who cannot keep themselves alive. Posterity will serve him; future generations will be told about the Lord. They will proclaim his righteousness, to a people yet unborn—for he has done it (Psalm 22:27–31).

When we thank God, we get out of our own self-oriented world. A biblical lament does not stay individualized for long. If I am praying for my healing, I should eventually pray for the healer to touch all those who are sick. If I am persecuted, I pray for my protection and faithfulness as well as those suffering more than me. *What are you thanking God for?*

Helping Someone in an Unexpected Trial

Understanding laments helps us minister to others when they face the most difficult trials. We can listen to their stories, encourage and join them in their feelings, ask questions that help them explore their desires, wait with them as they examine themselves, contemplate how God has worked in the past, and help them find what to thank God for in their current situation.

To allow a person to lament is to trust that God is at work even in the dark and painful times. Not everything has to be perfect, polished, and theologically precise. We cry, shout, question, remain silent, and wrestle through our thoughts and feelings—trusting that God is faithful to guide us. When we can walk alongside someone who is lamenting, we show them that we trust that God is with them. We avoid the simple clichés and trite responses that help avoid the pain of suffering. We face our own discomfort in not having all the right answers and join the person in their trial.

When Jesus faced the overwhelming burden of the cross, He chose one passage of Scripture to shout with His dying breaths—a lament psalm. He cried out, "My God, My God, why have you forsaken me?" (Psalm 22:1). Some gathered did not understand what He was saying, but I am sure that many others mentally surveyed the entire psalm and found a prayer of brutal and painful honesty, as well as a prayer of faithful hope and expectancy. In the trials we face, may our laments show the same honesty and faithfulness as our Lord's.

Questions to Ponder and Discuss

1. Why do you believe it is so difficult to identify the "real" problem when we are going through a trial? Describe an example of how you have misdiagnosed a problem in your life.

2. Read Psalm 37:4. In what way does this verse affect how you make your requests during a time of suffering? Does this verse imply that we should never pray for our own desires? Why or why not?

3. When examining ourselves, we can go to two extremes: exaggerating the role of sin in our lives or exaggerating our innocence and victimization.

To which extreme are you most vulnerable? Give an example from your own life.

4. Cite an example of how God has worked (in Scripture, in the life of someone you know, or in your own past) and how that example could help you when facing a future trial.

5. Job referred to his friends as "miserable comforters." Describe what makes you a good comforter to people who are suffering. What do you need to improve to be a more compassionate helper when someone is going through a trial?

Recommended Reading

When God Doesn't Make Sense by James Dobson
Between a Rock and a Grace Place: Divine Surprises in the Tight Spots of Life
    by Carol Kent
The Land Between: Finding God in Difficult Transitions by Jeff Manion

The Journey Continues … Our guess is that you may need to reread the previous chapter several times to grasp the multiple implications of pain and suffering. But you can be guaranteed that God will be growing you and your faith in the process. The seasons of growth are not always painful, but they require commitment. Let's look into those times of life when God ramps up your learning curve on the journey.

11

Later Seasons of Life:
Understanding the New Normal

Harry McFarlin

*Acceptance of a major transition in a believer's life
is the evidence of a living faith,
enhanced by spiritual maturity.*

Life is a series of transitions—from childhood to adolescence, from school to career—through all the changes that unfold during adulthood. Most of these changes are predictable; they're simply parts of our maturing process. However, the transitions we experience in midlife and beyond are a little different. They begin to limit our activities and the expectations we have of ourselves. They sometimes leave us in situations that in younger years we would have called devastating. This stage of life is what I've started calling "the new normal."

Glen Martin, the senior pastor at Journey of Faith, is a good friend of mine. He's several years younger than I am, so I always enjoy telling him about the joys of aging and "the new normal." We laugh about it often—and have been doing so for years—but I'm sure he's watched some of my transitions and wondered, "Will I have to go through this too?"

My goal in this chapter is to give each of you hope for reshaping your approach to the transitions of midlife and older life—to enable you to see the delight in "the new normal" and, most of all, to live an encouraged, vital Christian life through it all.

Reshaping Our Approach to Transitions

My office overlooks a parking lot and several apartment buildings. So when I gazed out one March morning, I was drawn to how the buildings needed paint and the parking lot needed to be cleaned up. A terrible way to begin the day! However, my mind slipped back to a recent day when my wife, Donna, and I had walked along the ocean. Nimbostratus clouds made their way northward after a light shower, and the warmth of the early-morning sun made me think about the approach of summer. Outside my window, as I noticed the wind was whipping the awnings into a frenzy, I recalled that the same wind the day before had provided just the right amount of air to lift the oddly shaped kites so that they soared over the heads of many beachgoers. I remembered watching a pod of dolphins as they bobbed through the surf that day. The scene in my memory was a far cry from the one in front of me, where a multitude of dirty papers cluttered the parking lot across the street and the paint was peeling from the buildings nearby.

Considering the contrast between the coarseness that confronted me with the beauty of God's creation enabled me to have a different perspective on life. You see, transitions may be wonderful or they may be painful. They may leave us with greater wisdom, or they may leave us somewhat incapacitated. We do not get to choose our transitions, but we can choose how we approach them. If you tend to be a parking lot gazer or an apartment paint critic, you will find your thoughts are often self-centered and discouraging. However, if you can approach a major life change by reflecting on the beauty that God brings to your life, then these times of transition begin to reveal their own beauty. In doing so, you can draw comfort and encouragement from the "new normal."

Solomon writes in Ecclesiastes that "He [God] has made everything beautiful in its time" (Ecclesiastes 3:11). Notice carefully that God did not simply make everything beautiful. He made everything beautiful *in its time*. It is at these "times" in life when everyone who is middle aged and older needs to reshape their approach. Transitions that might otherwise inspire panic or fear should instead be recognized as a product of God's grace and perfect timing—changes that are intended to reshape our physical and spiritual lives.

In just the last six years, I have experienced my own older-life transitions: two hip replacements, bypass surgery, and a current diagnosis of slow-growing, non-Hodgkin's lymphoma. These transitions have made major changes in my life and thoughts. I live today with a "new normal" that I find is filled with both peace *and* excitement.

Peace and Excitement in the New Normal

Scripture teaches us that God expects our faith in Him to generate both peace and excitement as we face the changes He allows. One of the most memorable accounts is found in Acts 12. Herod had murdered James, the apostle John's brother, and arrested Peter. Talk about a dire circumstance! Peter should have been climbing the walls or groveling in anguished prayer. Nope, the Bible says he was "sleeping." And listen to the sleeping arrangements: "The night before Herod was to bring him to trial, Peter was sleeping between two soldiers." Hold it! James has been killed; Peter has been arrested, thrown into prison, and positioned between two soldiers.

Somehow, that doesn't seem to lend itself to a tranquil night of sleeping. What's more, the passage notes that Peter had been "bound with chains" and that sentries (that's plural) were on guard outside his cell.

I have found myself in pretty bad circumstances, as I'm sure you have, and reclining in sleep in the midst of it has been almost impossible. Peter, however, was so relaxed that he didn't awaken when the cell filled with light and the angel of the Lord appeared. The angel had to actually strike him on his side and yell, "Quick get up!"

Can you imagine being that relaxed when in the midst of a major trial? Possibly you're like me, the last one to realize that God is doing something great in your life. Sometimes, it takes a good swift kick to wake me up. Reshaping our approach to transitions allows us to realize, take comfort in, and even derive a sense of excitement about the fact that, in this change, God is doing something great. My life may never be the same, but that doesn't mean it won't be a much better life.

Seeing the Delight in the New Normal

Fireworks displays on the Fourth of July each year never fail to enthrall me and many others across our nation. They represent the celebration of years of growth from a few colonies to a great nation of fifty states. Birthdays are often a time for reflection. And we can reflect on America's birthday that our growth as a nation has not come without pain and hardship. But the sacrifices of many generations, through several wars and a great depression, have left us with a bounty that exceeds every other nation in the world.

The history of our nation offers a vivid illustration of the progress that can come about with change. Each one of America's major transitions established another new foundation for discovery—from production of the Model A Ford in the early 1900s to the recent presentation of the iPad 2. Think about how far these periodic "new normals" have brought us. It is only when we view these things broadly that we realize the awesomeness of our great nation.

Recognizing the awesome power of change and its purpose from God's perspective is not new, but is seen over and over in the Bible. One such illustration is found in the gospel of Matthew, chapter 17. The Scripture tells us that "after six days Jesus took with him Peter, James and John, the brother of James, and led them up a high mountain by themselves. There He was transfigured before them, His face shone like the sun, and His clothes became white as the light" (Matthew 17:1–2).

As Jesus revealed Himself in the glory that was His, the apostles were also transformed. Their transformation, however, was internal. How could one stand in the presence of God's glory and not be forever changed? The passage goes on to speak of how they felt terror at what they were seeing until Jesus "touched them. 'Get up,' He said, 'don't be afraid' " (Matthew 17:7b). They raised their eyes, and the Bible says, "When they looked up, they saw no one except Jesus" (Matthew 17:8). Talk about an awesome and spectacular event! This was a major transition in the lives of these men, and the results produced changes that would be a major part of these men's lives and writing in the future.

Some of you, right now, are going through some deep valleys. Some of you are struggling to climb another hill. Many people have placed worldliness over godliness and now find themselves spiritually bankrupt.

The celebration of our nation's birth occurs once a year, and we take the many changes throughout America's history for granted. Most in each generation are impressed only with the changes that happen in their lifetime. God allowed us a moment when we too realized His holiness and actually saw His glory as it was revealed on the cross when He died for our sins and rose three days later from the grave. But it doesn't end there. Many of us take for granted the transitions in our lives and never see the awesome power of God in those changes. These changes are designed by God to allow us to grow in our faith. Some of them are exceedingly hurtful to go through; others are a joy and a pleasure. But they can all help us to grow in our faith, and that is something to be celebrated! "Look up and see Jesus" so that you can truly appreciate the new normal that comes with each transition.

Living the Christian Life of Encouragement

A friend once asked me why so many Christians walk around looking like they're sucking oatmeal through a straw. I don't know if that's true of most believers. But it certainly describes those who, while going through hard times, have forgotten the abundance of God. That abundance is ours in every situation. Consider Psalm 65. God has the psalmist portray for us a word picture of His finest work on our behalf. He encourages us through His provision of this earth and its abundance:

> You care for the land and water it, you enrich it abundantly. The streams of God are filled with water to provide the people with grain, for so you have ordained it. You drench its furrows and level its ridges; you soften it with showers and bless its crops. You crown the year with your bounty and your carts overflow with abundance. The grasslands of the desert overflow; the hills are clothed with gladness. The meadows are covered with flocks and the valleys are mantled with grain; they shout for joy and sing (Psalm 65:9–13).

These words renew my perspective. They remind me that God is providing and that He is enriching my life in every circumstance. Whether we reside on the plain, in the grasslands of the desert, or even in the valleys, we are blessed and enjoy continual provisions.

When you walk through the valley, do you "shout for joy and sing"? Are the hills you climb surrounded with a rejoicing spirit? How about the path you are on right now? Most of my journeys through life's valleys have been less than joyful. I usually find some reason to complain or blame someone else for my problems. After all, the problem couldn't be me!

My hills, come to think of it, don't always resonate with a rejoicing spirit, either. Sometimes, just the walk up tires me out, and it's easier to look at my feet and count each step as I climb the hill than it is to pause and let God's spirit maintain His song in my heart.

This wonderful psalm is offering all who love and worship God an alternative to natural human reactions of worry, fatigue, and despair. It suggests that our natural reactions can be supernatural if we allow the Spirit of God in our deepest valleys, on our highest hills, and, yes, even on the very path we are walking today, to refresh us with His Spirit, encourage us with His abundance, and actually bring His joy and song to our hearts as we let our transitions testify to His greatness.

Some of you, right now, are going through some deep valleys. Some of you are struggling to climb another hill. Many people have placed worldliness over godliness and now find themselves spiritually bankrupt. All of us need look no further than the first four verses of Psalm 65 for the answer:

> Praise awaits you, O God, in Zion; to you our vows will be fulfilled. O you who hear prayer, to you all men will come. When we were overwhelmed by sins, you forgave our transgressions. Blessed are those you choose and bring near to live in your courts! We are filled with the good things of your house, of your holy temple (Psalm 65:1–4).

Every one of the blessings and joy of the rest of the psalm belongs to the person who is willing to come before God, overwhelmed with sin, and ask forgiveness.

Living the Christian life of encouragement is allowing the refreshment of God to pour through our words and deeds and to touch others with His abundant grace as we move through some very hard transitions. "You answer us with awesome deeds of righteousness, O God our Savior, the hope of all the ends of the earth and of the farthest seas" (Psalm 65:5).

Living the Christian Life of Vitality

In writing about mid- and later-life transitions, I chose the word *vitality* because it has three slightly different definitions, and all of them apply to our transitions. The first is used to depict liveliness and is described as the "abundant physical and mental energy, usually combined with a wholehearted and joyous approach to situations and activities." The second is durability, which is "the ability of something to live and grow or to continue in existence." The third use of the word pertains to a vital principle that "distinguishes the living from the nonliving," according to Encarta Dictionary.[52]

All three of these definitions should help us understand what the Christian life is to look like from God's perspective. That life isn't limited to youth or young adults but is the basis for our identity as Christians. It is a life energized by the Holy Spirit, based upon living, eternal truths that will endure until God calls us home.

It is this truth that allowed the apostle Paul to write the following in his letter to the Philippians:

> Rejoice in the Lord always. I will say it again: Rejoice! Let your gentleness be evident to all. The Lord is near. Do not be anxious about anything, but in everything, by prayer and petition, with thanksgiving, present your requests to God. And the peace of God, which transcends all understanding, will guard your hearts and your minds in Christ Jesus (Philippians 4:4–7).

There can be tremendous disappointment when we realize we are no longer young, when we find ourselves transitioning into a "new normal" called midlife or older adult. This disappointment can easily undermine the great lesson of vital living that Paul wrote in the above passage.

In his book *Half Time,* author Bob Buford comes to a wise conclusion for those transitioning into midlife and older life. "The key to a successful second half is not a change of jobs; it is a change of heart, a change in the way you view the world and order your life."

I have found Mr. Buford's conclusion to be evident in the lives of many of the men and women whom God uses mightily in Scripture: Abraham, Moses, David, Naomi, and many others. Over and over, we see people whose hearts are aflame for God. These are men and women who are willing to see the world from God's eyes and are willing to reorder their lives to conform to God's desires. They set before us an example of living vitally for God.

How does that affect you and me as we live through midlife and older-life transitions? When I consider Abraham, the reality of a living faith confronts me and carries me through the trials I face. The life of Moses keeps before me the realization that I am human and prone to mistakes, but also that God in His perfection never fails. David's life challenges me to see that living through transitions is a growing experience in my spiritual life. Naomi's choices in life help me make decisions under pressure. They also help me to accept by faith the wonderful plan God has for me. These examples and many others keep before me the truth that God has provided a vital Christian life, and it is my responsibility to live it out as thoroughly as possible.

The Vitality of Humor

Do you have a sense of humor? Midlife and older-life transitions can be extremely challenging. Physical problems limit our natural abilities. Economic transitions, such as retirement, limit our financial abilities. Problems in the lives of our grown children challenge our strength and sometimes our finances. Donna and I have found that both of us rely heavily on our senses of humor to keep life in perspective.

In 2005, I suffered a heart attack and had five-way bypass surgery. Afterward, a nutritionist made it clear to Donna and me that if I wanted to continue to live, I would need to maintain a special diet low in sodium, fat, and cholesterol. My dear wife has limited her cooking since the children departed. Most things she prepares are delicious, but they are heated, microwaved, or fried. About a week after coming home from surgery, I suggested that the local bookstore might have some books on cooking for healthy hearts. She agreed, and after searching our local Borders, we found several. After spending about a half an hour reading the different recipes, she came out of the store. As she joined me in the car, I said, "Well, what do you think." Looking at me with her most serious expression, she said, "I think you're going to die." At this we both burst out laughing, which was very likely the healthiest thing I could have done for my heart.

Humor is an important part of vitality. It goes a long way toward ensuring a "joyous approach to situations and activities." We confront each transition with our frail, human character. We need to keep in mind that healthy progress occurs when we are able to laugh at ourselves.

The Vitality of Acceptance

The hardest part of any transition is accepting the change that it brings. My love for body surfing in the ocean has never diminished, but my ability to body-surf safely has been lost in the transition of midlife to older life. One of my last experiences at this sport came about two years ago. Spending most of my childhood and adult life enjoying the closeness of the Pacific

Ocean has taught me to respect but not fear its power. On this eventful day, I made my way out to where the waves were breaking. After waiting for just the right wave, I began to swim toward the beach. The mind of a body surfer at this moment is that of waiting with anticipation for the curling wave to lift and propel you toward the waiting sand. It was perfect! As I neared the shore, I tried to regain my feet and instantly realized that I had lost all equilibrium. I was so dizzy, I could barely stand up. Just then, the next wave hit me from behind and sent me to my knees. Fortunately, I wasn't alone. My son and son-in-law saw my dilemma and immediately rushed to my side, lifted me to my feet, and helped me ashore—obviously a rather inglorious ending to a lifetime of joy for this California native.

There is a passage in Ecclesiastes where Solomon writes about God preparing us for the change:

> Remember your Creator in the days of your youth, before the days of trouble come and the years approach when you will say, "I find no pleasure in them"—before the sun and the light and the moon and the stars grow dark, and the clouds return after the rain; when the keepers of the house tremble, and the strong men stoop, when the grinders cease because they are few, and those looking through the windows grow dim; when the doors to the street are closed and the sound of grinding fades; when men rise up at the sound of birds, but all their songs grow faint; when men are afraid of heights and of dangers in the streets; when the almond tree blossoms and the grasshopper drags himself along and desire no longer is stirred. Then man goes to his eternal home and mourners go about the streets (Ecclesiastes 12:1–5).

Solomon reminds us that the dimming of our senses, the wearing out of our teeth, and the fading of our hearing are all a part of life. These are not something he, or we, will take pleasure in as they occur. However, the vitality of the Christian life challenges us to accept these transitions and to continue to experience the presence and power of God in them.

In the gospel of Luke we find the great vitality of acceptance in our Lord at the time His greatest transitions were occurring. Having finished His teaching at the Last Supper and leading the disciples to the Garden of

Gethsemane, Scripture says, "He withdrew about a stone's throw beyond them, knelt down and prayed, 'Father, if you are willing, take this cup from me; yet not my will, but yours be done' " (Luke 22:41–42). We cannot read any of the Gospel accounts of the Crucifixion without realizing that Jesus accepted this limitation as His Father's will. It is in these moments in our own lives that the word *vitality* takes on its most meaningful definition, that of distinguishing "the living from the nonliving." The vitality of acceptance in the Christian life allows our faith to excel in hope.

Acceptance of a major transition in a believer's life is the evidence of a living faith, enhanced by spiritual maturity. It is a faith that accepts God's grace to its fullest extent. It realizes change is inevitable, but senses, going into that change, God's presence and power and in a Christ-like manner says, "Father, if you are willing, take this cup from me; yet not my will, but yours be done."

Today, I stand on the shore and watch the body surfers catching the waves. In my memory, I can actually feel the thrill of the moment as the body is pushed by all the power of the sea toward the shore. I enjoy it for them and cherish the memories. But then I reflect upon "the new normal" and see God working in many ways through my life. Just as surely as Jesus's death transitioned into the resurrection, so also do we transition into the newness of life.

I said at the beginning that my purpose was to give you a hope to reshape your approach to the transitions of midlife and older life. Finding delight in the new normal will enable you to live an encouraged, vital Christian life through it all. My words alone will not accomplish this. By taking a fresh look at your approach to transitions and making a commitment to enjoy the new normal, you can allow encouragement and vitality to define who you are in Christ.

Questions to Ponder and Discuss

1. List at least three transitions in your life that had a definite effect on your spiritual growth as a Christian.

2. Have you ever felt like running away from a problem? How did you cope with it? Did you find God in that instance or did you turn to

some other source of comfort and aid? How did that work out for you?

3. What is the "key" to transitioning through midlife according to Bob Buford? What would that key unlock for you in your life?

4. Do you hide the light of your Christianity? How can you share your faith with others without blinding them to the truth of Christ? How would sharing your faith help you grow through this transition in life?

5. What five qualities identify nonmediocre Christians? How many of these qualities do you have, and how can you gain the qualities you're missing?

Recommended Reading

Conformed to His Image by Kenneth Boa
Renovation of the Heart by Dallas Willard
Take Back Your Life by H. Dale Burke

The Journey Continues ... Before you start questioning, "What about the seasons of grief, or success, or leadership, or servanthood, or sacrifice, or loss, or ...," please recognize that we cannot examine every scenario in every season: a book has its limitations. However, one area we must briefly examine is the whole idea of eternity as the final and longest season of life. Fast-forward your life to the end and read the following pages to remind yourself that the journey never really ends.

12

The Journey into Eternity

Glen Martin

*Well, if heaven is real - and it is -
let's use Scripture as a guidebook to prepare us
for our eternity.*

Philip Yancey, writing in *Christianity Today*, noted that although 71 percent of Americans believe in an afterlife, no one talks about it much. "Percentages don't apply to eternity, of course; but for the sake of argument, assume that 99% of our existence will take place in heaven. Isn't it a little bizarre that we simply ignore heaven, acting as if it doesn't matter?"

Yancey points out that year after year, the *Reader's Guide to Periodical Literature* contains few, if any, articles devoted to the subject of heaven. There are many articles devoted to old age, death, and out-of-body experiences. But unlike previous eras, few books or magazine articles deal with heaven. Why? Yancey suggests three reasons:

1. The affluence we enjoy today has given us what former generations longed for in heaven.
2. A creeping paganism invites us to accept death as the culmination of life on earth.
3. Older images of heaven, the biblical ones, have lost their appeal. Streets of gold, pearly gates, and walls of emerald, sapphire, and jasper may have inspired Middle Eastern peasants, but they don't mean much to those living in the beauty of Southern California.

Yancey concludes, "To people who are trapped in pain, in economic chaos, in hatred and fear—to these, heaven offers a promise of a time, far longer and more substantial than this time on earth, of health and wholeness and pleasure and peace. If we do not believe that, then, as the Apostle Paul noted, there is not much reason for being a Christian in the first place."[53]

But there is a reason to believe and anticipate our final home as believers. Unfortunately, at a time when all truth is supposedly equal, much confusion and fear permeate our world and sometimes our theology. Does everyone go to heaven? Where is heaven? What will life be like when I get there?

Two Options for Eternity

The thought of heaven—and even the possibility of the opposite—has been a topic of conversation and consternation for thousands of years. It was one of those hot topics the very first disciples struggled to understand in light of what they witnessed in their earthly conditions. So our Lord said the following to the disciples in Luke 6:20b–23:

> "Blessed are you who are poor, for yours is the kingdom of God. Blessed are you who hunger now, for you will be satisfied. Blessed are you who weep now, for you will laugh. Blessed are you when men hate you, when they exclude you and insult you and reject your name as evil, because of the Son of Man. Rejoice in that day and leap for joy, because great is your reward in heaven. For that is how their fathers treated the prophets."

It's as though our Lord wanted the disciples to desperately grasp the notion that—for believers—this life pales in comparison with the one still to come. But there is another side to the coin. In contrast, look at the continuation of the story in Luke 6:24–25: " 'But woe to you who are rich, for you have already received your comfort. Woe to you who are well fed now, for you will go hungry. Woe to you who laugh now, for you will mourn and weep.' " Here, there appears to be a coming "balancing of the scales." The righteous who have suffered and lost and lived without will be blessed beyond measure in heaven one day. And the unrighteous and unsaved who have prospered and enjoyed the good life at the expense of others and at the expense of their relationships with God will have a very different view of eternity. Let's look at the two options.

Option One: Heaven

I love to see history and, therefore, love to travel. One of my favorite aspects of traveling is the preparation: reading the history, looking at maps, and examining the guidebooks. Preparation is invaluable, because without it, you have no idea what to expect. Yet by far the most important piece of advice I can give you is the need for a passport. No passport—no travel! Heaven has a similar qualification for entrance. To enter the gates of glory, your entry fees and visas were all paid by the blood of Jesus Christ, the Son of God and the Savior of the world. When Jesus died for our sins, was buried, and rose from the grave, every person was given the opportunity to receive the greatest gift ever offered humanity ... forgiveness for our sins and eternal salvation. And once your passport is secured, you have to be ready for new customs, different food, assorted languages, and even some new people. Thorough preparation makes the journey less scary and much more enjoyable. Well, if heaven is real—and it is—let's use Scripture as a guidebook to prepare us for our eternity.

Heaven Is a Real Place. For starters, let's dismiss all those mental pictures of people with wings floating on clouds and playing harps, bored to death. Heaven, at the core of biblical teaching, is a real, physical place. The very familiar John 14:2–3 tells us, " 'In my Father's house are many rooms; if it were not so, I would have told you. I am going there to prepare a place for you. And if I go and prepare a place for you, I will come back and take you to be with me that you also may be where I am.' " Revelation 21 describes heaven as a visible location with visible structures made of visible materials with real dimensions and measurements. We've all heard of streets of gold and pearly gates and jewel-encrusted walls. These are physical descriptions of a real place. And let me dare to say something about another physical description I wrestle with. Revelation 21:1–2: "Then I saw a new heaven and a new earth, for the first heaven and the first earth had passed away, and there was no longer any sea. I saw the Holy City, the new Jerusalem, coming down out of heaven from God, prepared as a bride beautifully dressed for her husband."

It appears that just as human beings experience death, a bodily resurrection, and complete transformation, so will our planet. Why would God go to all the trouble of creating the Earth only to throw it into an incinerator at the conclusion of history? I am more and more convinced that at least a part of heaven will be here on Earth—after a stunning transformation.

Heaven Promises No More Suffering. This is a big issue because many people suffer in life and experience the evil of this world and wonder (1) if God even exists, and (2) if He does exist, why life has so much pain. Here's the problem: we want every season of our life's journey to be a good season, and life just isn't like that. But I can guarantee this: you will live happily ever after if you are a Christian! One of my favorite verses in the Bible is 2 Corinthians 4:1: "Therefore, since through God's mercy we have this ministry, we do not lose heart." With all Paul had gone through, how could he say that? But he doesn't say it once; he says it twice. In 2 Corinthians 4:16, he says, "Therefore we do not lose heart. Though outwardly we are wasting away, yet inwardly we are being renewed day by day." Even in the midst of Paul's outward wasting away—probably during his older years—he knew something very important, as is described in 2 Corinthians 4:17–18: "For our light and momentary troubles are achieving for us an eternal glory that far outweighs them all. So we fix our eyes not on what is seen, but on what is unseen. For what is seen is temporary, but what is unseen is eternal." What did Paul know that we evidently don't? No suffering, no glory. Romans 8:17: "Now if we are children, then we are heirs—heirs of God and co-heirs with Christ, if indeed we share in his sufferings in order that we may also share in his glory." There it is: no suffering, no glory. You wonder why you're suffering? Glory! God has promised those who suffer that He will be glorified by imparting His honor to us and sharing it with us because of what He purchased for us on the cross. "Well," you may say, "Glen, that doesn't make suffering any easier." It does if the glory overshadows our present suffering. You see, the beauty of Romans 8 is not that God creates the glory: the beauty is found when God *reveals* the glory. Evidently, it's already there. Romans 8:18: "I consider that our present sufferings are not worth comparing with the glory that will be revealed in us." God uses suffering to change us and prepare us for service so we can be ready for the joy in heaven. So instead of a radical, all-at-once transformation *when* we arrive in heaven, God starts the process now.

If you really want to look forward to heaven, you have to start breaking free from the media-imposed limitations and perceptions of your future home.

Heaven Is a Community. Throughout human history, God has demonstrated His desire to be in relationship with His creation. Scripture tells us He walked in the Garden of Eden with Adam and Eve. God knew Moses face to face. He often spoke verbally to the prophets. And guess what? We have been made in God's image, longing for this relational component of life. When God created Adam, He couldn't stand the thought of Adam being by himself. In Genesis 2:18, the Lord God said, " 'It is not good for the man to be alone. I will make a helper suitable for him.' " Heaven will be the ultimate fulfillment of this community we long for because we will be in God's presence and hanging out with people who arrived there before us. Want to talk politics with George Washington? Have at it! Want to play catch with the Christian baseball players of old? No problem. You can chat with any Christian from times past or grab lunch with the apostle Paul. You will be reunited with all your Christian family who are already there. You will recognize them, and they will recognize you. Imagine seeing Mom and Dad again. Or spending time with your grandparents or the mate whom you have missed for so many years. Imagine those first few minutes of hugs and smiles after years of separation. In Matthew 22:2, God says it will be like a big party: " 'The kingdom of heaven is like a king who prepared a wedding banquet for his son.' "

Heaven Won't Be Boring. Heaven is a busy place. Some Christians fear boredom in heaven. They worry that they are going to be incredibly content but have nothing to do. Some have portrayed disembodied spirits floating from cloud to cloud, singing favorite songs, playing harps, and living eternity in prayer. Friends, our ultimate home is not cloudy, not boring, and not lacking passion. When you get to heaven, you will have so many options, you will have trouble choosing what you want to do first. And all the options will make you happy. You will experience new colors, new sounds, new feelings, and new experiences. I believe you will get to explore other places, other cities—even other galaxies. The early church fathers were so convinced of this, Augustine once wrote, "we will have such bodies that we will be [able to go] any place, where and when we want."

If you really want to look forward to heaven, you have to start breaking free from the media-imposed limitations and perceptions of your future home. You will have so much to learn. Remember, God is infinite, and you will never fully understand all there is to know about Him. But think about the fun of trying to fully comprehend His enormous power and character. And don't think you won't have work to do. We have already learned that it was God who created work by His very acts of creation. In describing heaven, the apostle John says in Revelation 22:3, "No longer will there be any curse. The throne of God and of the Lamb will be in the city, and his servants will serve him." For some of you, work is a pain, and the thought of work continuing in heaven is more painful. Work and service in heaven will be fun and energizing because you will be contributing and making a difference in eternity. That's how God made you.

Heaven Without End. Heaven is endless. How do you define *forever*? Living in this finite existence, words such as *forever* and *infinity* and *eternity* seem beyond comprehension. Not in heaven. In heaven, you will experience the following:

1. Eternal happiness. No more tears. No more crises in the family. No more fear of job loss. No more hoping and praying the checkbook will balance. Can you even imagine eternal happiness from God's point of view?

2. Eternal health. Heaven is a place where your body will no longer experience the decay of life. There are no cancer centers. CVS does not dispense prescriptions. Doctors do not take appointments. Tests are never ordered. You will be healthy forever.

3. Eternal relationships. From cover to cover, the Bible has given you instruction on living a relational life—an eternal relationship with God and eternal relationships with others. Never again will you experience the pain of a severed relationship. No more breakups, funerals, or the guilt of wondering what more you *could* have done.

4. Eternal life. For Christians, there is much more to the journey of life than the seventy to eighty years we may spend on this planet. Within every human heart is a homesickness for the perfect life of Eden. All of us long for what Adam and Eve essentially threw away because of their disobedience.

Heaven is a real place to be experienced in a real way. Jesus told the disciples, " 'And if I go and prepare a place for you, I will come back and take you to be with me that you also may be where I am' " (John 14:3). Simple words with eternal ramifications!

Option Two: Hell

You are in the process of becoming one of two kinds of people. One group has accepted Jesus Christ as Savior and will be in heaven one day, experiencing unbelievable beauty and peace. Another group will be in hell. Matthew 13:41–42 warns us, " 'The Son of Man will send out his angels, and they will weed out of his kingdom everything that causes sin and all who do evil. They will throw them into the fiery furnace, where there will be weeping and gnashing of teeth.' " You will either become a loving child of God, as God originally intended, or a twisted, angry person who rejects the love of Jesus. There is no in-between or neutral position here. You will either be a creature of heaven or face the worst nightmare ever imagined. Let's answer a few questions you may have about option two.

Question 1: "What does the existence of hell say about the nature of God?" "Is God some kind of sadistic tyrant who gets a kick out of sending people to hell?" Please remember that nobody wants people to spend eternity in heaven with God as much as God does. Nobody anguishes over your lost family member or friend more than God. John 3:17 says, " 'For God did not send his Son into the world to condemn the world, but to save the world through him.' " The word *world* here is a reference to human beings. Jesus Christ came to save people. When Paul wrote to Timothy urging everyone to pray for those in authority, listen to what he said in 1 Timothy 2:3–4: "This is good, and pleases God our Savior, who wants all men to be saved and to come to a knowledge of the truth."

God paid the ultimate price so that people could be saved from a destiny of hell and death. In our world, if we really don't want people to do something, we have a way of urging them not to do it. We say, "You'll do that over my dead body!" Well, Jesus says to the human race, "If you want to go to hell, you'll have to go over my dead body" because that's the only way to get there. If you want to go to hell, you're going to have to walk all the way around the cross, because the cross represents a literal crossroads in human history. This is not a subject to ignore in the belief that you will get another chance to consider it when you get your last breath. The idea that anyone here today or anyone you know will spend eternity separated from Him breaks God's heart.

Question 2: "Why do people go to hell?" "If God is all-powerful, all-loving, and died for the sins of everyone, why do people end up in hell?" The short answer is this: God takes human freedom and our ability to choose with the utmost seriousness. He created us in His image to be free people because only free people are truly able to love. John 3:18–21 explains it further:

> "Whoever believes in him is not condemned, but whoever does not believe stands condemned already because he has not believed in the name of God's one and only Son. This is the verdict: Light has come into the world, but men loved darkness instead of light because their deeds were evil. Everyone who does evil hates the light, and will not come into the light for fear that his deeds will be exposed. But whoever lives by the truth comes into the light, so that it may be seen plainly that what he has done has been done through God."

Our Lord says, "Light has come into the world, but men loved darkness." Paul was very direct in addressing the state of "lost" people when he wrote the following in Romans 1:21–25:

> For although they knew God, they neither glorified him as God nor gave thanks to him, but their thinking became futile and their foolish hearts were darkened. Although they claimed to be wise, they became fools and exchanged the glory of the immortal God for images made to look like mortal man and birds and animals and reptiles. Therefore God gave them over in the sinful desires of their hearts to sexual impurity for the degrading of their bodies with one another. They exchanged the truth of God for a lie, and worshiped and served created things rather than the Creator—who is forever praised. Amen.

Did you catch the phrase *God gave them over*? That phrase, one word in the original language, is one of the saddest in the New Testament. It means "to hand over" or "relinquish control" of something. Here's the answer: God will say to people, "Have it your way, the way you want." Do you see that God, in His humility, makes it possible for people to reject Him? You can actually look to heaven and say, "I don't want you to be my God.

I don't want you to order my life. I don't want to be a part of your family, the church. Leave me alone." And ultimately, God will say, "Okay!" If you ask long enough and hard enough, God will leave you alone—permanently and finally. And this is what the Bible calls hell. God will not violate your will or your choice.

Question 3: "Are there any details about hell?" People also ask, "Where is hell?" and "What will the temperature be there?" Here's the problem with today's audiences: many people get their ideas of hell from cartoons on TV and in newspapers. *The Far Side* comic strip is famous for its portrayals of hell. And suddenly, hell doesn't look so bad. So people begin to rationalize, based upon these pictures, "I'd rather be in hell with my friends than in heaven with a bunch of weird people." "Come on, hell may be a little warm, but at least there aren't going to be a lot of rules and harps and boredom." You cannot understand the pain and the heartache of hell unless you compare it with the wonder and peace of heaven.

You see, heaven is a place of uninterrupted community with God. Heaven will be a ceaseless exchange of love and service and joy and delight. Revelation 21:4 says, " 'He will wipe every tear from their eyes. There will be no more death or mourning or crying or pain, for the old order of things has passed away.' " We all long for that. But you will never find this sense of brotherhood and community in hell: I don't care what the cartoons or commercials may say.

One of the prominent words used by Jesus for hell is the word *Gehenna*. Matthew 5:30 says, " 'And if your right hand causes you to sin, cut it off and throw it away. It is better for you to lose one part of your body than for your whole body to go into hell.' " The word *hell* is the word *Gehenna*. I have driven through this place called Gehenna in Israel. It was actually a valley outside of Jerusalem where infant sacrifices had taken place. In Jesus's day, Gehenna was a constantly smoldering garbage dump and site for disposing of the bodies of criminals who had been executed. This image of hell is described in Mark 9:47–48: "And if your eye causes you to sin, pluck it out. It is better for you to enter the kingdom of God with one eye than to have two eyes and be thrown into hell, where 'their worm does not die, and the fire is not quenched.' " No one creates something for the garbage dump. It ends up there only when something goes wrong.

Let me tell you why this is important to grasp. Some people think God made heaven, and it was a good place, and God created hell in the beginning as a very bad place. Earth then becomes an in-between or neutral place. That's false. The Bible clearly teaches that what God created in the beginning was all good. But then came the fall, and everything seemingly fell apart. Romans 8:20–21 says, "For the creation was subjected to frustration, not by its own choice, but by the will of the one who subjected it, in hope that the creation itself will be liberated from its bondage to decay and brought into the glorious freedom of the children of God." Hell came about only because of the fall. First, Satan and his angels, the demons, fell. Then the entire human race fell. But hell was originally for the Devil and his demons. Matthew 25:41 says, "Then He will say to those on his left, 'Depart from me, you who are cursed, into the eternal fire prepared for the devil and his angels.' "

I will say that Randy Alcorn, founder and director of Eternal Perspective Ministries, does make an outstanding point when he shares, "The best of life on Earth is a glimpse of Heaven; the worst of life is a glimpse of Hell. For Christians, this present life is the closest they will come to Hell. For unbelievers, it is the closest they will come to Heaven."[54]

Question 4: "Why doesn't God give us a second chance?" In other words, after I die, why doesn't God say, "Last chance, Glen. Is that your final answer?" This concept comes from many people's fears. Maybe, maybe, there's a whole bunch of people in hell saying, "If only I had another chance." And God says, "Nah, you had your chance—too late now." Hebrews 9:27 says, "Just as man is destined to die once, and after that to face judgment, so Christ was sacrificed once to take away the sins of many people; and he will appear a second time, not to bear sin, but to bring salvation to those who are waiting for him." This is not a game. You have no idea how many chances you've received in life. But each of us is in the process of becoming a certain kind of person. Our lives have a kind of "moral trajectory." And God, who is omniscient, is able to judge that trajectory totally, wisely, and fairly. So God sees those people who will be unable to choose forgiveness and salvation.

You see, the Bible does not teach us that hell is full of people who long to repent and become godly. So, here's what happens. People see the wonder of creation and say "No." People go to church and hear the Good News of Jesus Christ and say "No." Maybe they pick up their Bible and read it once in a while and say "No." A friend tells them about forgiveness of sins in Christ, but they say "No." They may even sense the Holy Spirit trying to break through their hardened hearts to offer comfort and peace, but they again say "No." Eventually, they can't be reached. You can't reach them through joy or pain. Spiritually, this too is hell. So, that's where these people go: they had their chances. You see, God loves His creations. But He is also very concerned with sin and human wickedness, and we ought to be glad He is. The day is coming when God's rejection of human wickedness will be public, decisive, and utterly final.

People wonder, "Will there be fire in hell?" The Bible says "Yes." But this doesn't much matter to someone who has become so hardened that they don't care anymore. To dwell in heaven, to sing praises to God, to serve the King of Kings and Lord of Lords, to live with brothers and sisters—that would be torture for them. That's why author and lay theologian C. S. Lewis says, "The doors of hell are locked from the inside."

Living Life in Light of Eternity

Let's make a giant assumption. You believe in eternity, and your greatest desire is to spend forever in the presence of God. How does this decision change the way you live life now? Does this commitment to live your life in light of eternity change the way you parent, your attitude toward your career, or your use of time and money? I contend it will, and here is why. There are blessings that come from God as the natural result of a life lived well in light of eternity. Here are a few.

First, God promises a special reward for suffering. For all the suffering, losses, and persecutions you have experienced while alive on earth, you will be rewarded. Matthew 5:10–12 says, " 'Blessed are those who are persecuted because of righteousness, for theirs is the kingdom of heaven. Blessed are you when people insult you, persecute you and falsely say all kinds of evil against you because of me. Rejoice and be glad, because great is your reward in heaven, for in the same way they persecuted the prophets who were before you.' " What are those rewards? I have no idea.

But they must be really, really good because they come from a perfect Father in heaven who loves His kids. Suppose I promised you a hundred dollars every time you sacrificed a dollar. What would you do? Most of you are savvy enough to think, "Can I give you five dollars? How about ten dollars? This would be a great return on my investment." But most of us do not realize the return on our suffering or the return on sacrifice or the return on times of trial. Many of life's returns and rewards depend on the faith we have exhibited while alive. As Hebrews 11:1 says, "Now faith is being sure of what we hope for and certain of what we do not see." Your faith makes the promises of God as real as what you can see.

Second, your service has eternal benefits. Our Lord made it clear that heavenly treasures are much more valuable than earthly ones. Matthew 6:19–21 says, " 'Do not store up for yourselves treasures on earth, where moth and rust destroy, and where thieves break in and steal. But store up for yourselves treasures in heaven, where moth and rust do not destroy, and where thieves do not break in and steal. For where your treasure is, there your heart will be also.' " How do you store up heavenly treasures through service? You can help rekindle a desire to have a relationship with God in someone who has turned away from God. You can serve the needy and meet the needs of those less fortunate than you. Just being hospitable has an eternal effect, according to Matthew 10:41–42. So, invite others over for dinner to enjoy their company and lift their spirits. And when you do not feel like going to work on an early Monday morning, stop and reflect on the idea shared earlier: your vocation is holy unto the Lord. Unfortunately, we forget—especially when the pay is not "enough" or the working conditions appear to be unacceptable—that God rewards our labors when they are done as acts of worship.

One last reminder: greatness, in God's eyes, is found through servanthood. In Matthew 5:19, our Lord suggested that there will be differing levels of greatness in His kingdom. He says, " 'Anyone who breaks one of the least of these commandments and teaches others to do the same will be called least in the kingdom of heaven, but whoever practices and teaches these commands will be called great in the kingdom of heaven.' " Here's the problem: His standards of greatness are far different than ours.

His standards seem to teach that the way up is down and requires becoming a servant. Matthew 23:11–12 says, " 'The greatest among you will be your servant. For whoever exalts himself will be humbled, and whoever humbles himself will be exalted.' " Intellectually, I'm sure the disciples all agreed with Jesus's teaching, but the application of this instruction was traumatic. It was traumatic for them when Jesus washed their feet. It was traumatic for them when our Lord chastised them for not allowing the children to run to His side. Can you imagine the internal trauma when they watched the very Son of God arrested and willingly nailed to a cross for the sins of the world? And this very principle is what our Lord wanted modeled and taught because the little things matter to our Lord. It's often the apparently petty and unimportant things that have the greatest value to our Savior.

Conclusion

Heaven certainly will be a wonderful place filled with joy and brimming with community and worship. You never need to be afraid of going there! Consider the faith of a young couple in Owensborough, Kentucky, as told by their pastor, Jess Moody. One day the husband came to Pastor Moody's office clearly distraught and said, "Jess, I've just heard the most awful news. My wife has terminal cancer, and it has spread all over her body. The doctors have just told us she has only weeks, not even months, and Jess, she's at the hospital, and she's asking for you. We don't know how to handle it. We don't know what to do." Jess immediately went to the hospital. There the young wife and mother said to him, "I remember in one of your sermons you said a thousand years is like a day to God and a day is unto a thousand years. Is that true? Is a thousand years like a day to God?" The pastor said, "Yes, it's in the Bible." She said, "Good, because I've been doing the math, and I figure if a thousand years is like a day, then forty years is like one hour. I'll be leaving my husband and the children soon. He may live another forty years, but that will be just like an hour to me in heaven. When he gets to heaven, I'll greet him and say, 'Where have you been for an hour? Did you just go to the office, or were you running errands? I've missed you.' My children may live another seventy or eighty years, but that will be like two hours to me. When they get to heaven, I'll greet them and say, 'How was school today? Mom misses you when you're gone for a couple of hours. I wonder how you are doing, because mommies don't like to be away from their children long.' " Jess Moody said two weeks later she went to be with the Lord, and the last thing she said to her husband was "I love you. Take care of my children. I'll see you in an hour."

Now, that's an eternal perspective. It's the kind of perspective that should motivate each of us to live every moment for our Lord—until it's time to go home.

Questions to Ponder and Discuss

1. Over the years, people accumulate many erroneous ideas about heaven. What are some you have picked up on your journey of life? Where did you learn them?

2. Of the many descriptions of heaven provided in the New Testament, which one means the most to you and why?

3. Four significant questions about hell were answered in this chapter. Which of the four questions shed new light on your biblical understanding? What did you learn?

4. Why do you believe that "choice" is such a big deal to God? What would life be like if God had never given us free will? What responsibility do you have because of the freedom God has given you?

5. How should a chapter like this motivate you? Can you think of a couple of people in your sphere of influence who may need to read this chapter? Stop and pray for them by name, asking our Lord to provide you the opportunity to talk to them about what you have learned.

Recommended Reading

Heaven by Randy Alcorn
The Glory of Heaven by John MacArthur
In Light of Eternity by Randy Alcorn

13

Epilogue

Glen Martin

*If you have read this book without
allowing your soul to catch up to your body,
it has been a wasted exercise.*

An American traveler had planned a long safari to Africa. His journey had been consumed with the urgent issues of life, and rarely had he taken time to think about meaning and purpose. He thought a safari would be just what the doctor ordered: wide open spaces, fresh air, new surroundings, and plenty of free time. One problem: he was a compulsive man, loaded with maps, timetables, and agendas. Nothing was going to slow him down. To help transport all the gear he believed necessary for this trek, he hired local villagers to carry the supplies, luggage, and his other "essential stuff." Once all the preparations had been completed, the team woke early to get a good start on the journey. They traveled quickly and went far. The next two mornings, they followed the same schedule, traveling as fast and as far as possible. The American traveler was pleased by the progress they made and failed to notice the weariness of his fellow travelers, who collapsed on the third evening. After breakfast the next morning, the tribesmen refused to move. They simply sat by a tree reclining in the coolness of the morning. The American traveler became incensed. Time is money, he fumed, and they were wasting his. So, he demanded to know what was going on. His translator smiled and told the traveler something very profound: "They are waiting for their souls to catch up with their bodies."

If you have read this book without allowing your soul to catch up to your body, it has been a wasted exercise. In our fast-paced culture, we are often like the American traveler, searching for meaning in the "doing" side of life. And when the doing side is providing just enough fulfillment to keep us motivated, we hope the "being" side of life will be equally fulfilled. That is not the case. From God's perspective, we need to walk in what He has already declared us to be. Our being should be centered on Him, in Christ's completed work on the cross and what transpired at the moment of salvation. We not only received forgiveness and the hope of glory, but received and continue to receive much more. We receive everything we need to walk successfully in the Christian life. We are complete in Christ and can tap into and enjoy all the fullness of God's Spirit dwelling in us and helping us to become all that God created us to be.

There is a book in your Bible neatly tucked away, about two-thirds of the way through the Old Testament, called Ecclesiastes. Written by the second-smartest person to have ever walked the Earth, (after the Lord Jesus Christ) it appeals to the young to heed the warnings of an older man who has grown, matured, and learned how to prepare others for the journey of life. Solomon speaks of successes and frustrations. He tells of all the ways in which he tried to make something of his life and of all the reasons why the question "What does it all mean in the long run?" was never really answered from a human perspective.

Like many a rich man, Solomon gave himself to pleasure, drinking, carousing, and sampling all the other distractions money can buy. Ecclesiastes 2 shares the breadth of his personal debauchery:

> I thought in my heart, "Come now, I will test you with pleasure to find out what is good." But that also proved to be meaningless. "Laughter," I said, "is foolish. And what does pleasure accomplish?" ... I denied myself nothing my eyes desired; I refused my heart no pleasure. My heart took delight in all my work, and this was the reward for all my labor ... Then I turned my thoughts to consider wisdom, and also madness and folly. What more can the king's successor do than what has already been done? (Ecclesiastes 2:1–2, 10, 12).

God has built within every person some basic needs and desires, which when followed, will help you discover your worth in the eyes of God and your purpose on the Journey of Life.

If there had been a qualified counseling center in Jerusalem 2,500 years ago, Solomon might have found a seat on a couch. There, he might have said, "I'm just not happy with my journey of life. I feel like I am missing out on true meaning and purpose. I've tried it all. I've done it all. With all the advantages I have had, where did I go wrong?" And from any good therapist, Solomon would have heard this response: "Why are you being so hard on yourself? Be realistic; lower your expectations! After all, you're only human." And Solomon would have left the tidy little office even more disappointed, knowing this was not the advice he needed. Solomon, like so many others, set his goals high, hoping to do something influential and important with his life.

This is why Solomon asks the question "What makes life matter? Is there more to life than doing all you do and being forgotten when you're dead?"[55] Solomon, disappointed by his personal journey, had failed to recognize the significance God could play in his life. I am in no way saying Solomon was ignorant of the need of God. God shares the following in Ecclesiastes 3:11–13:

> He has made everything beautiful in its time. He has also set eternity in the hearts of men; yet they cannot fathom what God has done from beginning to end. I know that there is nothing better for men than to be happy and do good while they live. That everyone may eat and drink, and find satisfaction in all his toil—this is the gift of God.

Solomon's conclusion was a gigantic leap of faith that allowed his soul to catch up with his body. Your relationship with God determines your success and significance on life's journey. Secular culture measures success and significance by results and achievements. Did you win or lose? Did you succeed or fail? Did you show a profit or loss? God alone can judge us on the basis of *who we are*, not *what we have done* (1 Samuel 16:7).

Basic Human "Beings"

In my book *Beyond the Rat Race*, I suggest God has built within every person some basic needs and desires, which when followed will help you discover your worth in the eyes of God and your purpose on the journey of life.

Be Helpful. Our human nature is such that we need to be helpful and thoughtful when it comes to the needs and concerns of others. I contend that this is just as valuable as eating, sleeping, and exercising. When we eat too much or exercise too little, we feel out of sorts, and we can forget what it's like to feel good. Helping others is part of our nature also, and when this core value is not allowed to express itself, we feel empty inside.

Do you remember the story of Joseph in the Old Testament? When Joseph was seventeen, he was sold into slavery by his jealous brothers. His comfortable, secure life as "Daddy's favorite" abruptly ended and was replaced with one filled with hardship and insecurity. For twenty years, Joseph must have dreamed of the day when he could get even with his brothers. He was willing to put up with loneliness and injustice while he anticipated the day his brothers would plead with him for mercy.

Then, one day, it happened. Famine struck the land of Canaan, and Egypt was the only place with a storehouse of grain. By then, Joseph had become the Pharaoh's minister of agriculture and was responsible for distributing this grain. His brothers and father would soon stand before him, and Joseph would have his opportunity for revenge. But this encounter was not nearly as enjoyable as he had dreamed. He discovered that the human soul is not made for jealousy and revenge: it is made for helping others. Joseph not only forgave his family for their abuse and neglect, but made sure they were given a place to live in the finest area of Egypt, the land of Goshen.

Be Honest. God has given every person a conscience. It tells us many things about how we should act even when we are not yet in relationship with God through Jesus Christ. One of the personal attributes hot-wired into the human soul is honesty. We desire the trust of other people. Our conscience tells us we must be honest if we are to expect honesty from others. When we choose to ignore our conscience, the natural result is guilt. This is part of being created in the image of God. The closer we draw to God, the more important honesty becomes and the greater our desire to be absolutely honest in every area of our life.

Be Faithful. Being faithful runs counter to our tendency toward rebellion. But God is faithful and expects His children to be the same. We long to be labeled the "good and faithful servant," yet forget the commitment necessary to remain faithful. We forget how fulfilling and enriching faithfulness can be as a way of life. And nothing can do more to undermine trust and loyalty than failing in this area. Proverbs 28:20 reminds us, "A faithful man will be richly blessed, but one eager to get rich will not go unpunished."

Okay, we're finished. No, not with the journey of life, but with this book. Time for you to do the arithmetic I described in the first chapter. Maybe you can start to do the math with a simple prayer:

Lord, teach me to number my days, so I may have wisdom. I know You are not done with me, and I also understand You have given me breath and life to make a difference for You. Enable me to be faithful to Your calling, obedient to Your will, and caring to Your people. May I become the man/woman of faith You desire me to become as I enjoy and promote my Lord Jesus on this journey of life.

Questions to Ponder and Discuss

1. How often do you feel like the American businessman in this story? Share two events in the past week—events that illustrate the idea that your soul has not caught up to your body.

2. Read Ecclesiastes 3. What do the words of Solomon have to do with your personal journey of life?

3. Someone once said, "Some people don't go through life—they're shoved through it." Of course, this can be good and bad. It's good when you are pushed to finish something, or when you attempt something new and completely out of your comfort zone. But it's bad when your life is out of control, or when you allow other people's expectations to rule your life. Where are you on this continuum? What got you to this point in your life?

4. When all is said and done, the journey of life is actually a journey to know God. All human beings long for a spiritual awakening. Let's assume this is true! If so, why would a shift in our thinking to a more spiritual journey be worth more in the long run than simply living the "good life"?

5. What are you doing with your dash? I want you to close with probably the hardest, most compelling assignment in this book: write your own obituary. For what do you want to be known? What do you want people to be saying at your funeral when your journey is complete?

Recommended Reading

A Passionate Life by Mike Breen and Walt Kallestad
Soul Talk by Larry Crabb
Ordering Your Private World by Gordon MacDonald

Endnotes

1. Steven J. Lawson, Psalms 76:15 in the Holman Old Testament Commentary series edited by Max Anders (Nashville, TN: Broadman & Holman, 2006), 334.

2. A. S. Romer, *Man and the Vertebrates* (Baltimore: Penguin, 1933), 17.

3. William A. Dembski, *Intelligent Design* (Downers Grove, IL: InterVarsity, 1999), 234.

4. W. E. Vine, *An Expository Dictionary of Biblical Words* (Nashville, TN: Thomas Nelson, 1984), 125–126.

5. W. E. Vine, *An Expository Dictionary of Biblical Words,* 841.

6. Merrill C. Tenney, *The Zondervan Pictorial Encyclopedia of the Bible,* Vol. 2 (Grand Rapids, MI: Zondervan, 1975), 496–500.

7. US Census Bureau, Current Population Survey (CPS)—Definitions and Explanations, www.census.gov/population/www/cps/cpsdef.html, (viewed December 2010).

8. Jack O. Balswick, Pamela Ebstyne King, and Kevin S. Reimer, *The Reciprocating Self: Human Development in Theological Perspective* (Downers Grove, IL: InterVarsity, 2005), 211.

9. answers.yahoo.com/question/index?qid=20081008080557AAF8rYR (December 1, 2010).

10. Gary Thomas, *Sacred Influence: How God Uses Wives to Shape the Souls of Their Husbands* (Grand Rapids, MI: Zondervan, 2006), 23.

11. Jim and Sarah Sumner, *Just How Married Do You Want to Be?* (Downers Grove, IL: InterVarsity, 2008), 70.

12. Clifford and Joyce Penner, "Sparking the Ho-Hum Sex Life." *Focus on the Family Magazine*, March 2009. www.focus.org.nz/default. aspx?go=article&aid=439. Tara Parker-Pope, "When Sex Leaves the Marriage." *New York Times* blog, 3 June 2009. well.blogs.nytimes. com/2009/06/03/when-sex-leaves-the-marriage (April 13, 2011).

13. Florence Isaacs, *Toxic Friends, True Friends* (New York: Kensington, 1999), 48.

14. Donald Miller, *A Million Miles in a Thousand Years* (Nashville, TN: Thomas Nelson 2009), 48.

15. James Dobson, *Bringing Up Boys* (Carol Stream, IL: Tyndale House, 2001), 249.

16. Frances A. Schaeffer, *He Is There and He Is Not Silent* (Carol Stream, IL: Tyndale House, 1972).

17. James Dobson, *Life on the Edge* (Nashville, TN: Word Publishers, 1995), 41.

18. David Popenoe, *Life Without Father* (New York: Free Press, 1996), 191.

19. Gary Chapman, *The Five Love Languages of Teenagers* (Chicago: Northfield, 2000).

20. "Valparaiso Basketball Community Remembers John Wooden," n.d., www.valpolife.com/index.php?option=com_content&view=article &id=7724:valparaiso-basketball-community-remembers-john-wooden &catid=23:college-pro&Itemid=410 (January 12, 2011).

21. "Research Shows Parenting Approach Determines Whether Children Become Devoted Christians," April 2007, www.barna.org/family-kids-articles/106-research-shows-parenting-approach-determines-whether-children-become-devoted-christians (January 12, 2011).

22. K. S. Hymowitz, "Kids Today Are Growing Up Way Too Fast," October 1999, manhattan-institute.org/html/_wsj-kids_today_are_growing.htm.

23. Hymowitz, "Kids Today Are Growing Up Way Too Fast."

24. Deborah Tannen, *You're Wearing That? Understanding Mother/Daughters in Conversation* (New York: Random House, 2006).

25. Mary Beth Hicks, *Bringing Up Geeks* (New York: Berkley Books, 2008).

26. Walt Mueller, *Youth Culture 101* (Grand Rapids, MI: Zondervan, 2007).

27. "Sexuality, Contraception, and the Media," 2004, Center on Media and Child Health, www.cmch.tv/ (January 12, 2011).

28. "Teenagers in the United States: Sexual Activity, Contraceptive Use, and Childbearing," *Vital and Health Statistics,* 2004, Series 23, No. 24.

29. Mary Beth Hicks, *Bringing Up Geeks* (New York: Berkley Books, 2008).

30. Mary Beth Hicks, *Bringing Up Geeks,* 66.

31. D. Michael Lindsay, *Creating a Culture of Connectivity in Your Church* (Loveland, CO: Group Publishing, 2005).

32. C. S. Lewis, *The Lion, the Witch, and the Wardrobe* (New York, NY: HarperCollins, 1950), 64–65.

33. Lewis Smedes, *Shame and Grace. Healing the Shame We Don't Deserve* (New York, NY: Zondervan, 1993), 117, 153, 109.

34. J. I. Packer, *Knowing God* (Downers Grove, IL: InterVarsity, 1977), 41.

35. Gary Moon and David Benner, *Spiritual Direction and the Care of Souls* (Downers Grove, IL: InterVarsity, 2004), 107.

36. Robert Mulholland, *Invitation to a Journey* (Downer's Grove, IL: InterVarsity, 1993), 22.

37. Don Willett, *Stages of Faith* (1998 by Don Willett).

38. Richard Foster, *Celebration of Discipline: The Path to Spiritual Growth* (New York: Harper and Row, 1978), 1.

39. Paul Pettit, ed., *Foundations of Spiritual Formation: A Community Approach to Becoming Like Christ* (Grand Rapids, MI: Kregel, 2008), 21.

40. Chuck Swindoll, *So You Want to Be Like Christ? Eight Essentials to Get You There* (Nashville, TN: W Publishing Group, a Division of Thomas Nelson, 2005), 78.

41. Douglas Hyde, *Dedication and Leadership* (Notre Dame, IN: University of Notre Dame Press, 1992), 79.

42. William Temple, From *Readings in St. John's Gospel* (Peabody, MA: Morehouse Publishing, 1985).

43. Warren Wiersbe, *Real Worship* (Grand Rapids, MI: Baker Books, 2000), 48.

44. C.S. Lewis, "Blusphels and Flalansferes: A Semantic Nightmare," in *Rehabilitations* (1939).

45. A. W. Tozer, *Whatever Happened To Worship* (New York, NY: Christian Publications, 1985), 44–45.

46. Timothy Keller, *Counterfeit Gods* (New York, NY: Dutton, Penguin, 2009), Introduction.

47. Eugene Peterson, *A Long Obedience in the Same Direction* (Downers Grove, IL: InterVarsity, 2nd printing 2000), 54.

48. Bill Hybels, *Too Busy Not to Pray* (Downers Grove, IL: InterVarsity, 1988), 52.

49. Wayne Grudem, *Systematic Theology* (Leicester, England: InterVarsity, 1994), 1016.

50. Bill Hybels, *Christians in the Marketplace,* rev. ed. (Wheaton, IL: Victor Books, 1992), 12.

51. Nancy Guthrie, *Holding On to Hope* (2002 by Nancy Guthrie), 10–13.

52. http://encarta.msn.com/encnet/features/dictionary/DictionaryResults. aspx?lextype=3&search=vitality (December 13, 2010).

53. Philip Yancey, "Heaven Can't Wait," *Christianity Today,* September 7, 1984, 53.

54. Randy Alcorn, *Heaven* (Carol Stream, IL: Tyndale House, 2004), 28.

55. See Ecclesiastes 2:14–16.

CPSIA information can be obtained at www.ICGtesting.com
Printed in the USA
LVOW041832090911

245574LV00002BA/9/P